Indian Palmistry

A Short Treatise

Indian Palmistry
A Short Treatise

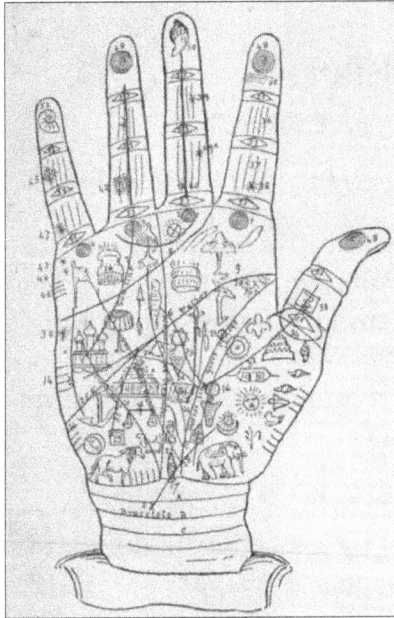

Nathaniel Altman

Gaupo Publishing
Brooklyn, New York
www.gaupo.net

GAUPO PUBLISHING

Indian Palmistry: A Short Treatise.

Copyright © 2020 by Nathaniel Altman

A portion of this material originally appeared in *The Little Giant Encyclopedia of Palmistry*, published by Sterling Publishing Co., Inc. in 1999.

Published in the United States of America
by Gaupo Publishing.

ISBN 978-0-9979720-6-1

Dedicated to the memory of
Rukmini Devi.

Table of Contents

Introduction

Indian palmistry, known as *Samudrika shastra*, can trace its origins back thousands of years. While the so-called Indian school of palmistry (some refer to it as "Hindu palmistry") is somewhat different from both Western palmistry and Chinese palmistry, many modern Indian hand analysts are using Western interpretations in their consultations. Some traditionalists argue that the gradual adoption of Western palmistry with its emphasis on psychology is a betrayal of the ancient roots of Indian palmistry.

In India, palmistry has always been viewed as a sacred science. The human hand is considered a special part of the body that reveals each person's unique *dharma,* or life path for this incarnation. The lines themselves are considered manifestations of the Divine. Early palmistry texts stress that the hand analyst- the individual who interprets the sacred signs on the hand- must adhere to a strict code of personal conduct and not only should achieve a deep practical knowledge of palmistry, but reach a high level of spiritual attainment as well.

Some traditional Indian religions teach that each individual soul experiences many incarnations, and that the circumstances of our present life are determined by our thoughts, words and deeds from previous lives. By the same token, it is taught that our future lives will be determined by what we do in *this* life: how we take care of our health, how we create and maintain our relationships with others, the type of work we do, the life skills we

1

develop, the moral and ethical choices we make, and how we unfold and express our innate spiritual nature.

Many Indian spiritual teachers believe that by developing self-knowledge, we can tap into the energy, talents and interests that we may have brought with us into our present life. As we deepen our self-understanding, we create our own future, not only in this life, but in future ones as well.

I was introduced to Indian palmistry by Rukmini Devi Arundale, the noted theosophist, parliamentarian, animal rights activist, dancer and choreographer while I was working at the international headquarters of the Theosophical Society, Adyar (Chennai) in 1976. In addition to theosophy, we shared a strong interest in vegetarianism and animal rights, and she was very supportive of a book I had written about vegetarianism, *Eating for Life*. After a dinner at her home, Rukmini offered to read my hands and commented on my long *Bandha rekha*, which corresponds to the heart line in Western palmistry. She told me that it indicated long life, which (at age 72) is yet to be determined.

Indian palmistry is one of the three major schools of palmistry, which include the Chinese school and the Western school, which is believed to have originated in the Middle East in what is present-day Iraq. It is hoped that this slim volume will create more interest in Indian palmistry, and inspire the reader to further study.

Nathaniel Altman
Brooklyn, New York

1. The Palm and its Characteristics

Many of the teachings regarding the size, shape, thickness and consistency of the palm are similar in Indian and Western palmistry.

The well-known Hindu palmist K.C. Sen listed the ten signs of a "good" hand in his book *Hast Samudrika Shastra*. Some reflect the different racial types who live in India today.

1. The hands are warm to the touch.
2. The skin color of the upturned palm is "like the sky before the dawn," or a deep pink.
3. When the hand is opened, the fingers are held close together without any opening between them.
4. The skin texture of the hands is shiny "as if they are oiled."
5. The consistency of the hand is full and thick, yet without being fleshy or soft.
6. The hands are neither too large nor too small in relation to the person's body size.
7. The nails are copper-colored.
8. The fingers are long. (As in Chinese palmistry, if the length of the middle finger is greater than the length of the palm, the fingers are considered long.)
9. The palms are broad rather than long and thin.
10. Under normal circumstances, the hands are dry to the touch, as opposed to damp and sweaty.

According to traditional Hindu palmists, other specific characteristics of the palm have individual meanings.

- Hard hands: strong willed; tenacious; good in business; likes to get up early in the morning.
- Soft hands: lethargic yet restless; loves luxury and comfort.
- Well-formed hands with long fingers (in men): wealth.
- Skinny hands with protruding veins on back of hands (on women): unhappiness
- Raised mounts on thick palms: charitable character
- Marked hollowness in the center of the palm: person will lose inheritance from parents: poverty
- Palm with very few lines: poverty

Hand Types

Many of the characteristics of hands are identical to those in Western palmistry. However, Indian palmists have sometimes offered different interpretations.

Rudimentary Hands

Rudimentary hands are not unlike elementary hands in Western palmistry. The rudimentary hand (Figure 1.1) reveals a basically squarish palm with short, stubby fingers. The hand itself tends to be fleshy and usually contains very few lines (the lines themselves tend to be strong and deep). They give the appearance of solidity and strength. Arch and loop fingerprints predominate, and skin texture is often coarse.

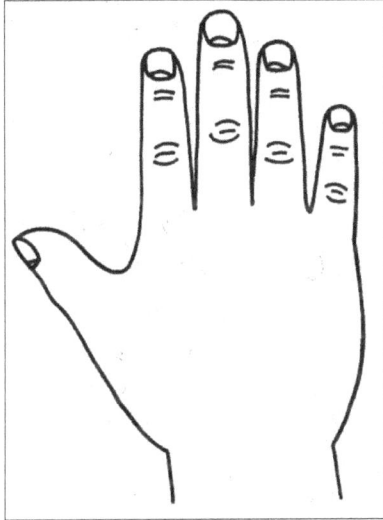

Figure 1.1. The Rudimentary Hand.

The vast majority of people with rudimentary hands are male, and they are often realistic, grounded in three-dimensional reality, and have the ability to function well in the material world. They tend to be deliberate, slow and practical, and prefer to see things in a simple, uncomplicated way. This is not an indicator of low intelligence, but rather a particular way of viewing the world.

For the most part, the owner of rudimentary hands dislikes change, and prefers a stable and predictable work environment with few, if any, surprises. Careers in agriculture, mining, work with heavy machinery and similar activities involving strong physical labor are popular. Rudimentary-handed people tend to be very attuned to nature, so they prefer to live and work in the countryside rather than in cities and towns. People with these hands are steady and reliable. They can also be conservative and set in their ways.

Square Hands

The *square hand* type (Figure 1.2) is recognized by its squareness in form as well as its squared-off fingertips. It is the hand of the organizer and planner.

- The hand is squarish in shape, with the palm and the fingers approximately the same length.
- The fingertips are often squarish in form.
- The nails are square, and slightly longer than they are wide.
- The fingers and thumb are firm and do not easily bend outward.
- The hand has a firm consistency.

Owners of this hand love order, method, and stability. Common sense rules their emotions, and they have a steady, systematic approach to life. They don't like confusion and often have difficulty adapting to new circumstances and situations, especially when the hand or thumb, or both, is rigid. They are often thorough, competent, and careful with money.

Often lacking in spontaneity, people with squarish hands like rules, methods, and structures. They like the "tried and true" and prefer to follow a fixed routine; they do not easily change, unless the hands are flexible.

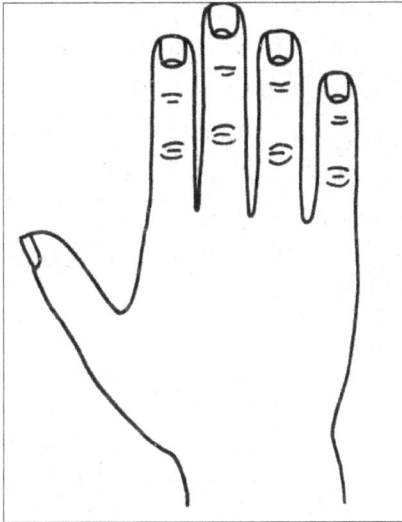

Figure 1.2. Square Hand.

People with squarish hands tend to be formal in their approach to relationship and are usually polite and reserved when dealing with others. They make excellent engineers, doctors, and bureaucrats. Square hands also give their owners an inordinate ability to persevere and to cope with difficult situations.

Indian palmists have depicted people with square hands as having a quiet temperament and an inquiring disposition. However, some believe that people with square hands are prone to mischief and can cause public scandal.

Spatulate Hands

Owners of *spatulate hands* (Figure 1.3) are often viewed as original and inventive. They are known for their restless and exploring personality.

- Spatulate hands are often broad and strong, with slightly knotted fingers.
- The fingertips fan out in the form of a spatula. The fingertip is often wider than the first phalange (the section from the base to the first knuckle).
- Broad nails are common.
- The palm is wider at the knuckles than at the wrist.

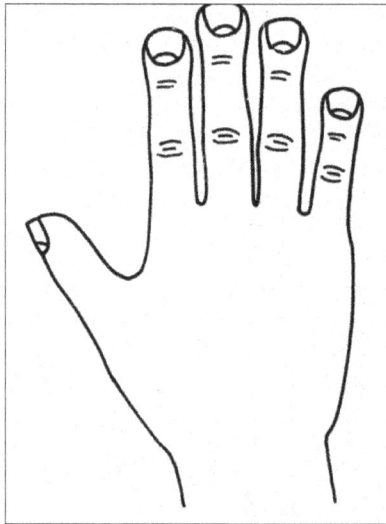

Figure 1.3. Spatulate Hand.

The best word to describe this hand is *action*. People with spatulate hands are energetic, tenacious, innovative, and self-confident. They are also independent, self-reliant, and curious about new ideas and see out unusual experiences. Like those with square hands, they are often practical and grounded in day-to-day reality.

Owners of spatulate hands tend to be creative and impulsive. They are generally extroverted, dynamic, and exciting to be with. They often have an uncanny ability to take advantage of a situation and use it to practical advantage.

Like the rudimentary hand, the spatulate hand is primarily sensate, and its owner favors activities on the material plane. Commerce, banking, construction, and entrepreneurship are popular areas of career interest for those with spatulate hands. People with spatulate hands are also good inventors and athletes. When flexible and pliable, however, a spatulate hand indicates an interest in sensual pleasure at the expense of work and other responsibilities.

In India, people with spatulate hands are seen to encompass a wide range of human behavior. On one hand, they are viewed as hard-working people who like to be on time. However, spatulate hands are also found on pleasure seekers.

Conic Hands

Conic, or artistic, hands (Figure 1.4) belong to people who are emotional, intuitive, and changeable. This type of hand is especially common among women.

- Conic hands tend to be slightly tapered at the base of the palm and at the tips of the fingers.

- The skin texture is usually fine, denoting sensitivity and a love of beauty.
- The hand has a soft yet springy consistency as well as a flexible thumb and fingers.
- In addition to the four major lines on the hand, there are usually a great number of finer lines, including many vertical lines.

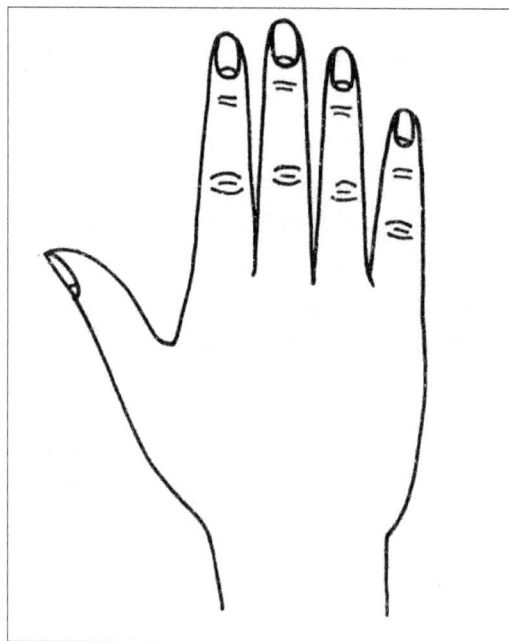

Figure 1.4. Conic Hand.

People with conic hands are governed by impulse and first impressions. Unlike those with squarish hands, who are ruled by reason, conic-handed people are sentimental, intuitive, impulsive, capricious and romantic.

Inconsistency is said to be a major problem with those who possess conic hands. They often begin a project with great enthusiasm, and then leave it for someone else to complete, especially if their hands are flexible. Although they tend to support the efforts of others, they shift loyalties often and have difficulty with commitment.

Creativity is high in owners of this hand. If the hand is firm and the lines well-formed, creative energies are channeled primarily toward intellectual pursuits. When the hand is bland and fat, there is a strong sensuous nature. Rich foods, money, abundant sex, and comfortable surroundings are counted among the primary needs of individuals of this hand type.

Conic hands are not highly regarded in India. Several authors have stated that people with conic hands are basically selfish and hungry for fame and recognition. As mentioned before, conic hands are said to reveal a sensuous nature, which of often frowned upon by contemporary societal standards, especially when applied to women.

Philosophical Hands

Hands with predominantly knotty fingers (Figure 1.5) reveal a "philosophical" person with a strong analytical mind. Their owners are rarely seduced by appearances and tend to penetrate deeply into an issue using logic, detail and analysis. On a psychological level, people with *philosophical hands* tend to lack spontaneity and find it difficult to express their feelings directly to others.

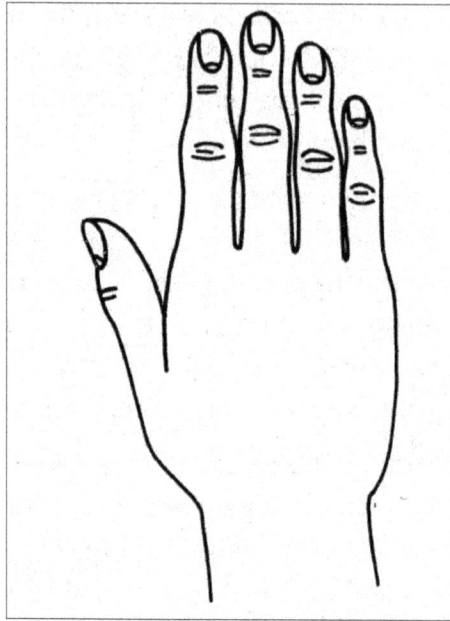

Figure 1.5. Philosophical Hand.

In India, individuals with philosophical hands are depicted as deep thinkers and seekers of truth. People with these hands (which appear to be more common in India than in Europe or North America) enjoy studying psychology, philosophy and metaphysics.

Mixed Hands

Very few hands actually conform in every detail to any one hand type in its purest form, although one type may predominate over the others. For this reason, Indian palmists have a fifth classification—the *mixed hand*, which can provide an important frame of reference for an accurate hand analysis.

By definition, the mixed hand (Figure 1.6) contains characteristics of two or more of the previous hand types. The hand may be primarily squarish, yet one or two fingers may be spatulate in shape. The overall shape of the hand may be conic, yet it also may contain elements found in the more practical square hand.

The basic shape of the hand should serve as the foundation of a careful hand analysis. The fingers, mounts, and lines- as well as modifiers such as hand consistency and size, skin texture, flexibility, and skin ridge patterns- can often provide more specific information regarding character analysis and individual life expression.

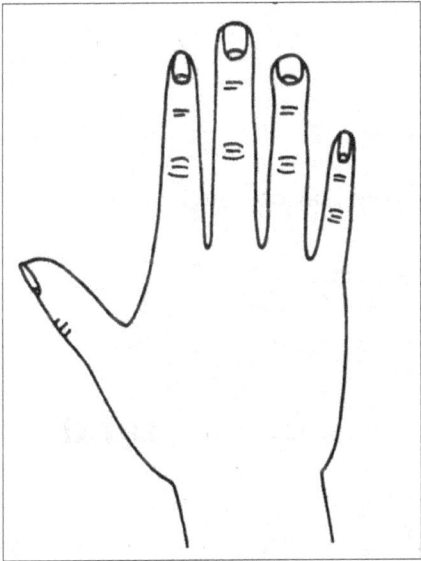

Figure 1.6. The Mixed Hand.

For these reasons, palmists tend to take all factors into account when studying a hand and evaluate the relationships among the various aspects. While this may appear daunting at first, you will eventually be able to achieve a thorough, balanced reading by cultivating intuition and patience. After some practice you will be able to recognize the basic "gestalt" of a hand after a few minutes of careful observation.

The Color of the Palm

Hindu palmists pay close attention to the color of the skin, especially on the palm of the hand. Taking into account that many Indian people have darker skin than Americans and Europeans, the colors have the following basic meanings:

- Red or pink color: good health, general good fortune
- Yellowish color: liver problems may be a sign of habitual sexual overindulgence
- Bluish color: Overindulgence in alcohol or drugs
- Whitish color: low energy; poverty

The Sthanas of the Hand

The Kartikeyan system of palmistry, which developed in southern India centuries ago, teaches that there are different regions of the hand (known in Sanskrit as *sthanas*, or "places", as seen in Figure 1.7) on which are engraved lines known as *rekhas*. Although both hands are important in Indian palmistry, hand analysts tend to focus on a man's right hand and a woman's left hand. However, the significance of certain markings may differ according to the hand on which it is found.

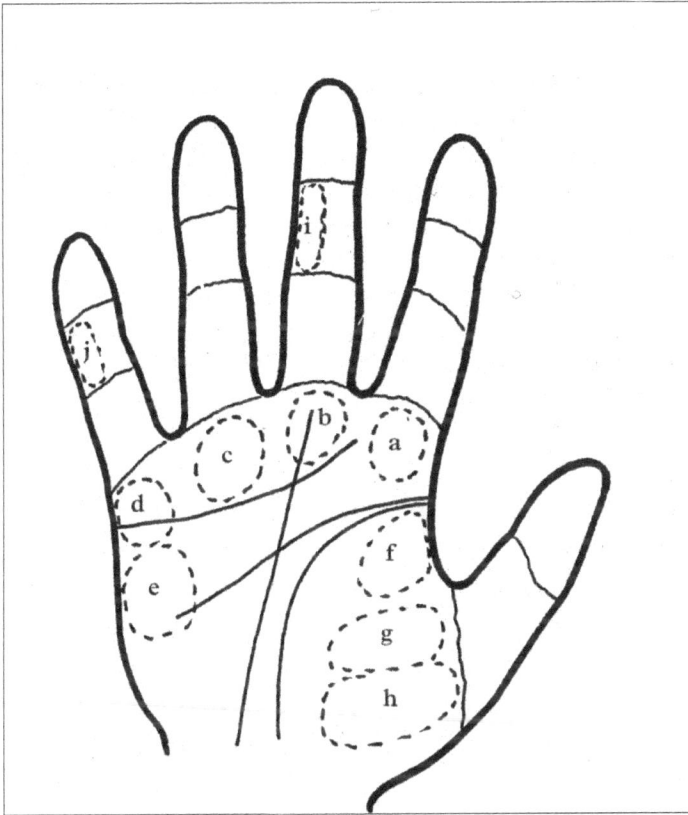

Figure 1.7. The Ten Sthanas of the Hand.

As part of the Indian school of palmistry, the Kartikeyan system teaches that there are ten basic regions of the hand and fingers. While most correspond to the mounts found in Western palmistry, their significance is often quite different. In contrast to the mounts in Western palmistry these sthanas usually do not have great significance in themselves. Rather, they are seen as a *blank canvas* on which distinct palmar markings offer important insights into the person's health, character and future endeavors. For this reason, most books about Indian palmistry follow the Western system of classifying the mounts according to different planets, such as Jupiter, Saturn or Mars. More often than not, they also provide interpretations that are similar to books written by Western hand analysts.

Pithru Sthana

The *Pithru sthana* (a) is located beneath the index (Jupiter) finger.

Mathru Sthana

The *Mathru sthana* (b) corresponds to the Saturn mount in Western palmistry.

Vidya Sthana

The *Vidya sthana* (c) is the pad located beneath the ring finger, corresponding to the mount of Apollo.

Jaya Sthana

The *Jaya sthana* (d) is in a location similar to that of the mount of Mercury in Western palmistry. It is located under the little finger.

Dharma Sthana

The location of the *Dharma sthana* (e) corresponds to what Westerners call the upper mount of Mars, located below the beginning of the heart line.

Sathru Sthana

The *Sathru sthana* (f) is found in the depression of the palm, which roughly corresponds to the lower mount of Mars in Western palmistry. The word "sathru" means "foe."

Brathru Sthana

This region, known in India as the *Brathru sthana* (the sthana of brothers) is located on the upper half of the thumb ball or Venus mount (g).

Bandhu Sthana

The *Bandhu stana*, or "the place of relatives," is found in the lower part of the mount of Venus (h).

In addition to the eight major sthanas found on the palm, Indian palmistry recognizes two additional sthanas on the middle and little fingers. The left half of the middle phalange of the middle finger is called *Putra Sankhya sthana* (i) or "the place of the number of sons," while the left half of the little finger (j) is called the *Putra sthana*, or "the place of sons."

In the following chapters, we will examine some of the dozens of markings found on the sthanas and explore their significance.

2. Fingers and Nails

A detailed study of the fingers and nails is very important to Indian palmists. Although many contemporary Indian hand readers ascribe the same qualities to the fingers and nails that Western palmists do, books that focus on traditional Indian or Hindu palmistry often offer very different interpretations- some appearing unusual or even extreme to Western readers.

In this chapter we will examine some of the traditional Indian interpretations of various aspects of the fingers and fingernails, taking into account the very different cultural and religious traditions found in this fascinating land.

Long, slender fingers with conic tips (Figure 2.1) have always been highly regarded in India. Many Hindu saints- such as Lord Krishna- are said to have possessed such hands.

However, on a practical everyday level, which involves holding down a job and sticking to a budget, these hands are far from ideal. They reveal an impractical individual who may have difficulty focusing on the material needs of others. However, for those who already have a source of steady income and wish to develop their artistic, intellectual or spiritual capacities, such a hand is perfect for them to have.

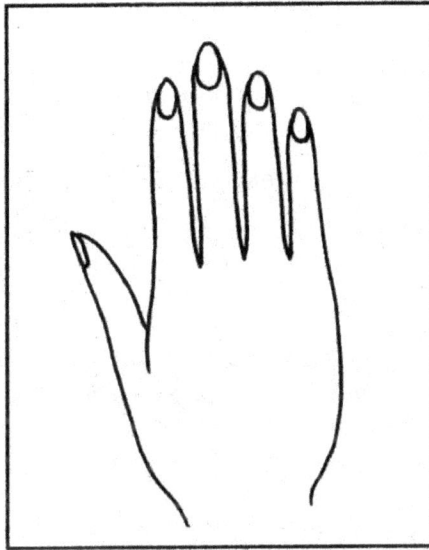

Figure 2.1. Conic hand with long, slender fingers.

Hindu palmists have offered the following observations regarding specific finger characteristics:

- Straight fingers: overall good fortune
- Fingers that are straight and long: long life; tendency to hide one's feelings
- Crooked fingers (on males): poverty
- Crooked fingers (on females): childlessness or widowhood
- Fingers that are thick and round: difficulty in handling money; poverty
- Fingers that are short and flat (with flat tips): low economic status; destined for menial jobs
- Dry fingers: low economic status

- Closed fingers (on open hand): wealth; ability to save money
- Gaps between the fingers (when fingers held together): poverty; inability to save money
- Gap between base of index and middle finger (Figure 2.2): careless; impulsive; unconventional

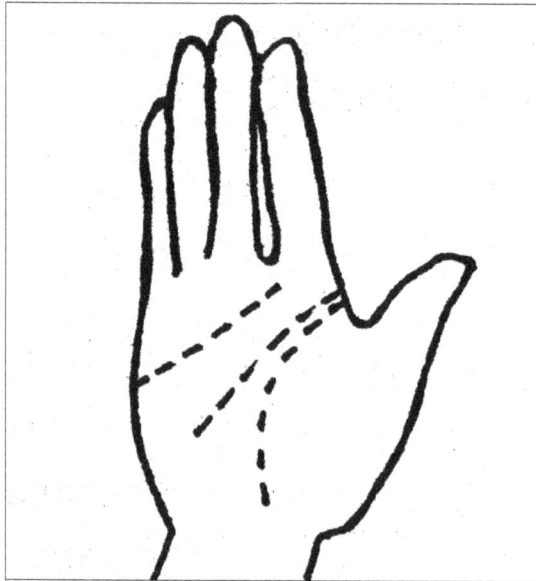

Figure 2.2. Gap between base of index and middle finger.

- A gap between base of the middle and ring fingers (Figure 2.3): unconventional personality; may lack discretion

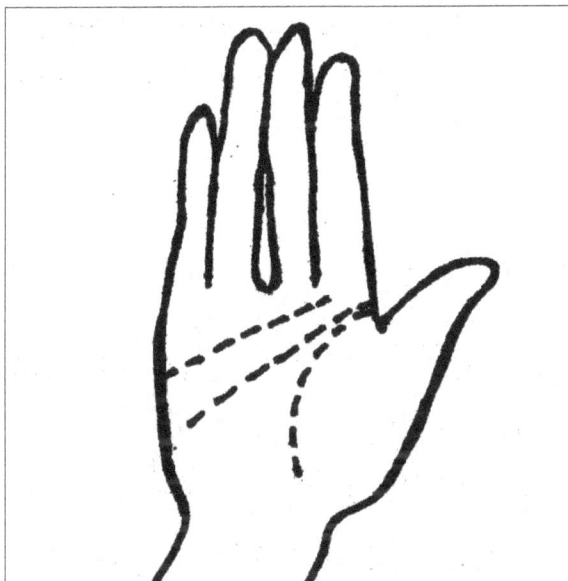

Figure 2.3. Gap between base of middle and ring finger.

- A gap between base of the ring and little fingers: headstrong and opinionated
- Fingertips bending back: tenacious nature
- Stiff fingertips that do not bend back: greedy
- Long top (mental) phalanges (Figure 2.4): ability to work skillfully with one's hands (such as carpenters, artists, hairdressers, surgeons, sculptors)
- Thin, weak lower (material) phalanges: shy, retiring personality
- Thick, fleshy lower (material) phalanges: tendency to overindulge in food and drink; greedy

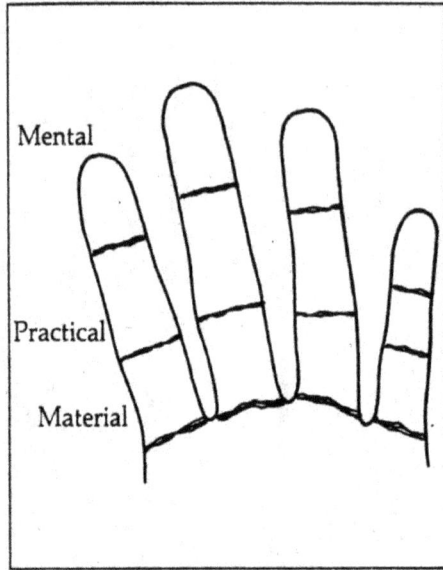

Figure 2.4. The phalanges of the fingers.

- Long little finger (reaching the top phalange of the ring finger): success through one's own efforts
- Extra fingers or partly formed extra fingers: poverty; troubles in relationships; possible short life

The Thumb

Traditional Indian palmists believe that the thumb is the most important finger on the hand. It is said that, in some parts of India, palmists focus their attention on the human thumb alone. Many of the Western interpretations regarding the thumb have been adopted by contemporary

Indian hand analysts. What follows are those observations that differ.

Generally speaking, traditional Indian palmists teach that the thumb should be relatively long and roundish; the upper and lower phalanges of the thumb should be of similar proportions; and the thumb tip should reach the middle (i.e. practical) phalange of the index finger.

People with this type of thumb are believed to possess a sound physical constitution and have a strong aptitude for higher education, especially in the fields of engineering, design and the sciences. By contrast, Hindu palmists believe that thumbs that are short, flat and crooked spell misfortune, whether in marriage, health of career.

- Low-set thumb (Figure 2.5): adaptable personality; independent; generous; intelligent
- High-set thumb (Figure 2.6): lower intelligence; rigid and narrow-minded personality
- Supple thumb (i.e. that easily bends back under pressure): trouble holding onto money
- Firm thumb: stable, reliable personality; strong will
- Stiff thumb (i.e. that doesn't bend back under pressure): greedy; rigid personality
- Small thumb (Figure 2.7): guided by emotions; lack of determination
- Large thumb (Figure 2.8) guided more by the intellect than by the emotions
- Round, strong, slightly flexible thumb: overall good fortune in health, marriage and career

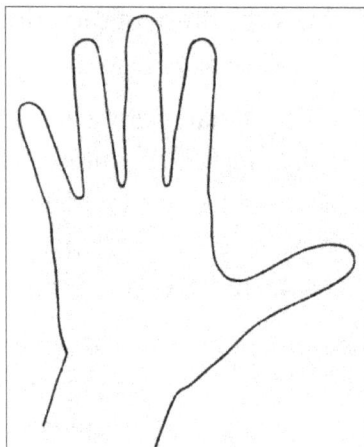

Figure 2.5. Low-set thumb.   **Figure 2.6. High-set thumb.**

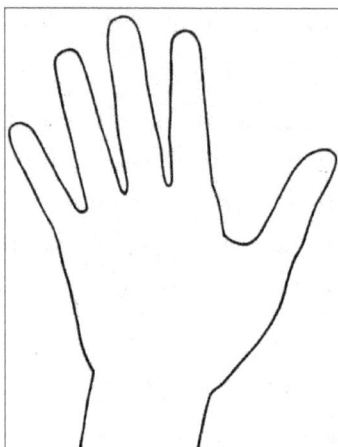

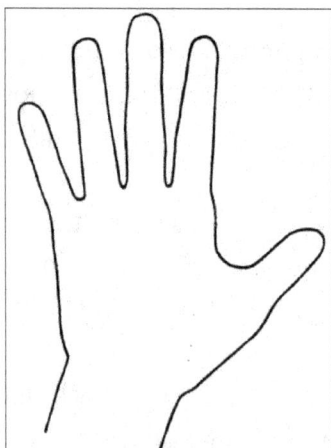

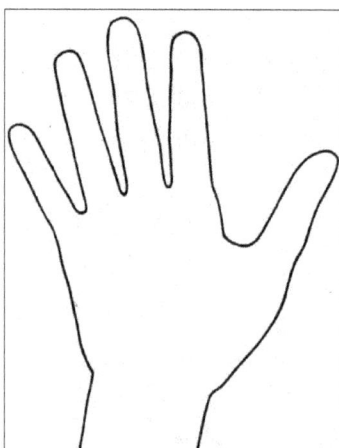

Figure 2.7. Short thumb.   **Figure 2.8. Long thumb.**

- Short thumb with a flat tip (Figure 2.9): prone to misfortune in all areas of life

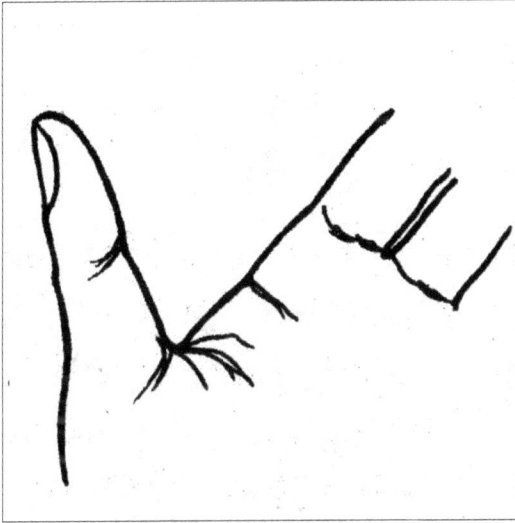

Figure 2.9. Thumb with flat tip.

The thumb has two phalanges or *parvas*, while the other fingers have three (Figure 2.10).

- Wide upper parva (on female hand): widowhood
- Wide upper parva (on male hand): bachelorhood
- Wide upper parva and "waisted" lower parva: argumentative nature; difficulties with relationships
- Long upper parva: self-reliant, strong will power
- Short upper parva: propensity for evil; difficulty in establishing and maintaining relationships with members of the opposite sex
- Conic fingertip: diplomatic nature
- Long and thick lower parva: logical thinker; easily grasps difference between right and wrong

- Short and thin lower parva: poor judgment; deficient intellect
- Thick lower parva: frequent travel
- Rounded, fleshy thumb (on female hand): will marry into wealth

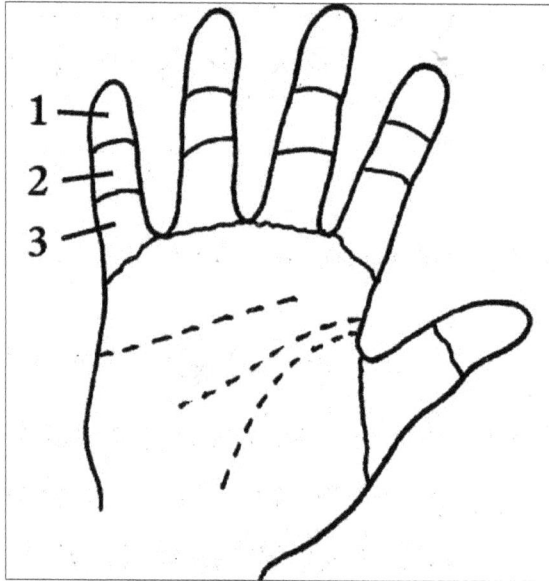

Figure 2.10. The parvas of the fingers:

1. Upper, 2. Middle, 3. Lower.

Other Fingers

Indian palmists generally ascribe the same qualities to individual fingers as Western palmists. However, different interpretations sometimes exist, especially in regard to personality and health.

Index Finger

- Index finger the same length as the middle finger: prideful nature; conceited; snobbish
- Crooked top phalange of index finger: potential for lung disease
- Index finger leaning towards middle finger: prideful nature

Middle Finger

- Very long: tendency towards glandular diseases
- Crooked top phalange: violent temper; tendency towards abdominal problems
- Conic top phalange: volatile, excitable character
- Middle finger leaning towards index finger: overly superstitious nature
- Middle finger leaning towards ring finger: increased optimism and cheerfulness

Ring Finger

- Ring finger same size as index finger: professional success in the arts and music
- Ring finger longer than index finger: strong artistic ability
- Ring finger the same length as the middle finger: sign of a gambler
- Crooked top phalange of ring finger: potential for scandal of a sexual nature

- Ring finger leaning towards middle finger: tendency to become sad and depressed

Little Finger

- Little finger whose tip reaches halfway up the top phalange of the ring finger: sign of intelligence and scholarly excellence
- Little finger that is the same length at the ring finger: sign of a genius IQ
- very short little finger (one whose tip does not reach the top phalange of the ring finger): paranoid tendencies; potential to remain sexually immature as an adult
- Pointed tip on little finger: potential for glandular problems
- Very small and deformed little finger (on female hand): poor ovarian function
- Little finger leaning towards ring finger: creativity in one's career

The Three Parvas

In addition to the "places" on the palm mentioned earlier, Indian hand analysts recognize the different phalanges of the fingers, known in Sanskrit as *parvas* (Figure 2.10). We discussed the parvas of the thumb earlier in this chapter, and will focus on the other fingers here.

According to Indian tradition, each parva should ideally be of equal length and of similar proportions.

- The top phalange or upper parva is said to represent the mental world
- The middle parva represents the material world
- The base phalange or lower parva reflects aspects of the sensual or material world

The longer the phalange of a particular finger- in comparison to the others- the stronger are the qualities that the parva represents.

- A long, well-developed upper parva on all the fingers is a sign of a person with high aspirations
- People whose middle parvas are well-developed tend to do a lot of thinking. They enjoy studying and investigation
- When the base of the lower parva is thick and long, the person loves the sensual pleasures of life, such as food, sex and luxurious surroundings

Long Upper Parva (Top Phalange)

- On index finger: strong emotions; sensitivity; the ability to be inspired and inspire others; when conic, strong religious devotion
- On middle finger: tendency to want to be alone; if bent towards ring finger: melancholy; if conic: excitable nature
- On ring finger: strong creativity, especially in art and design

- On little finger: good communicator; strong intuition, especially in mathematics, science and healing

Long Middle Parva

- On index finger: practical; ability to get things done
- On middle finger: works well on his or her own; good researcher and investigator; enjoys working with plants or machinery; talent for working with medicinal herbs
- On ring finger: ability to work in an artistic field, including interior design, landscape design or architecture; favors a career in music or theater; proficiency in working with ceramics
- On little finger: ability to work in areas of science, mathematics or healing; talent for business

Long and Thick Lower Parva (Base Phalange)

- On index finger: good business sense; enjoys luxury
- On middle finger: tendency to be greedy and acquisitive
- On ring finger: loves being surrounded by beautiful (and often expensive) things
- On little finger – long: shrewd; prone to dishonesty
- On little finger – thick: tendency towards overindulgence in food, alcohol and sex

Nails

Although long considered a reliable indicator of human character, the nails have also been believed by Indian palmists to be a clear barometer of the person's health.

Ideally, the nails should be slightly longer than they are wide, with a naturally shiny appearance. People who possess this type of nail are considered pleasant individuals who are also healthy and refined.

- Long nails (Figure 2.11): weak physical constitution; tendency for heart and lung diseases, especially when the nails are also curved and thin. On the positive side, they are also a sign of an open-minded individual who is tolerant of other points of view
- Long nails with whitish hue: person of good character; someone who can be relied upon
- Long, thick an curved nails: considered a sign of loose morals; tendency towards cruelty
- Narrow and long: shrewd personality
- Narrow, long and curved: prone to back problems
- Fan-shaped (Figure 2.12): back problems; throat diseases
- Short (Figure 2.13), thin and flat: tendency to be critical and quarrelsome; person is quick to anger; tendency towards heart disease
- Nails with white spots: highly strung; nervous personality
- White spot on thumb nail: love affair

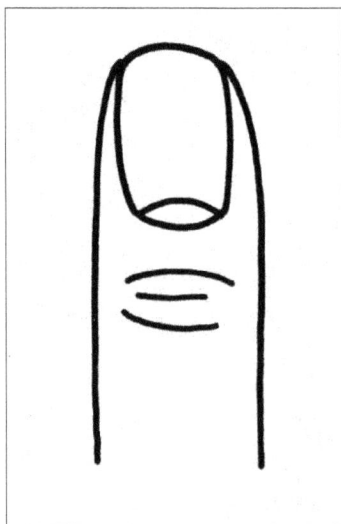

Figure 2.11. Long nail.   **Figure 2.12. Fan-shaped nail.**

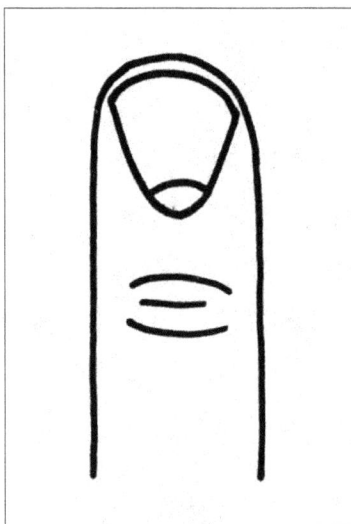

- White spot on nail of index finger: person will profit from a business deal
- White spot on nail of middle finger: upcoming trip by sea or air
- White spot on nail of ring finger: honors and wealth
- White spot on nail of little finger: success in business
- Nails with black spots: grief and misfortune
- Black spot on thumb nail: illicit love affair
- Black spot on nail of index finger: loss of wealth due to a bad business deal
- Black spot on nail of middle finger: premature death
- Black spot on nail of ring finger: scandal

- Black spot on nail of little finger: sudden death
- Beau's lines – deep furrows moving across the nail (Figure 2.14): a severe illness that has adversely affected the nervous system
- Nails with yellowish marks: impending death

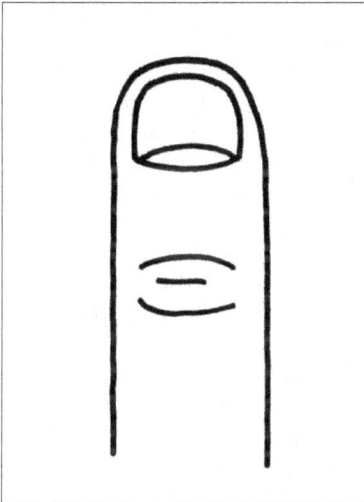

Figure 2.13. Short nail.

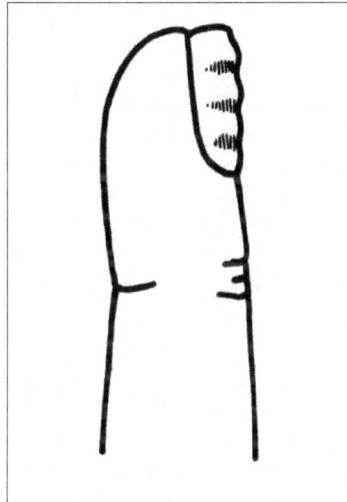

Figure 2.14. Beau's lines on nail.

3. The Major Lines

As in Western palmistry, understanding the significance of the various lines of the hand (known in India as *rekhas*) is essential to a careful hand analysis. Although some modern Indian palmists have adopted the Western meanings of the major lines, traditional practitioners consider these lines to have a different significance.

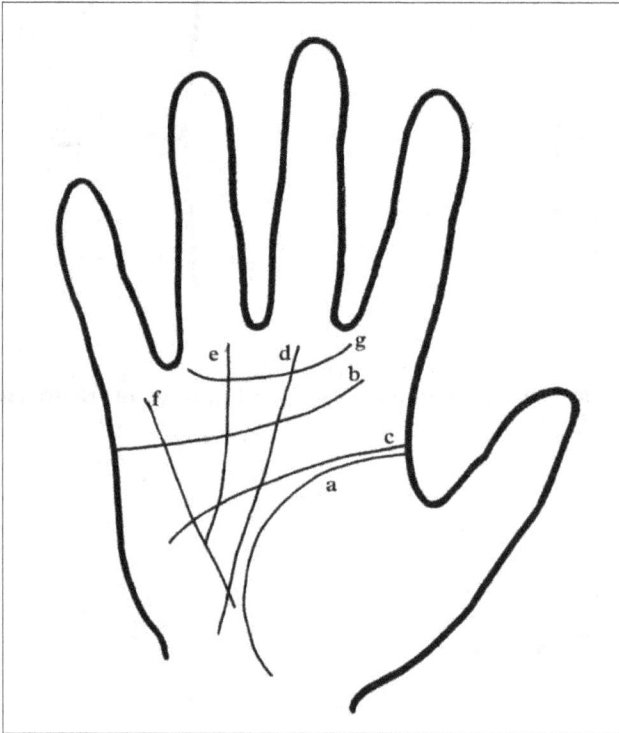

Figure 3.1. The Major Lines of the Hand.

a. Atma rekha b. Bandha rekha c. Dhan rekha
d. Indira rekha   e. Kamala rekha f. Bala rekha
g. Mandoshnada rekha

Hindu palmists have long taught that the left hand contains lines and markings that reflect our actions in past incarnations. In other words, the left hand shows our *inheritance* from previous lifetimes and what we are "born with" in this life. The right hand shows what we are making of our health, talents and personality traits we have inherited from the past.

The way traditional Indian palmists determine age in the hand is unique. According to custom, they measure a line on the hand with a piece of hair from an elephant's tail. When placed across the line, the width of the hair is said to be equivalent to one year of the person's life.

The method of gauging time through the lines of the hand tends to vary among individual hand analysts. One system was developed by Nitin Kumar, one of India's most respected palmists, as seen in Figure 3.2.

Line Quality and Color

Among Indian palmists, it is taught that clear, deep, pinkish and long lines are considered to be the best kind to have. They reveal:

- steadiness of purpose
- good health; strong physical constitution
- strength of character; courage

By contrast, weak, shallow and broken lines have more negative meanings:

- weak physical constitution

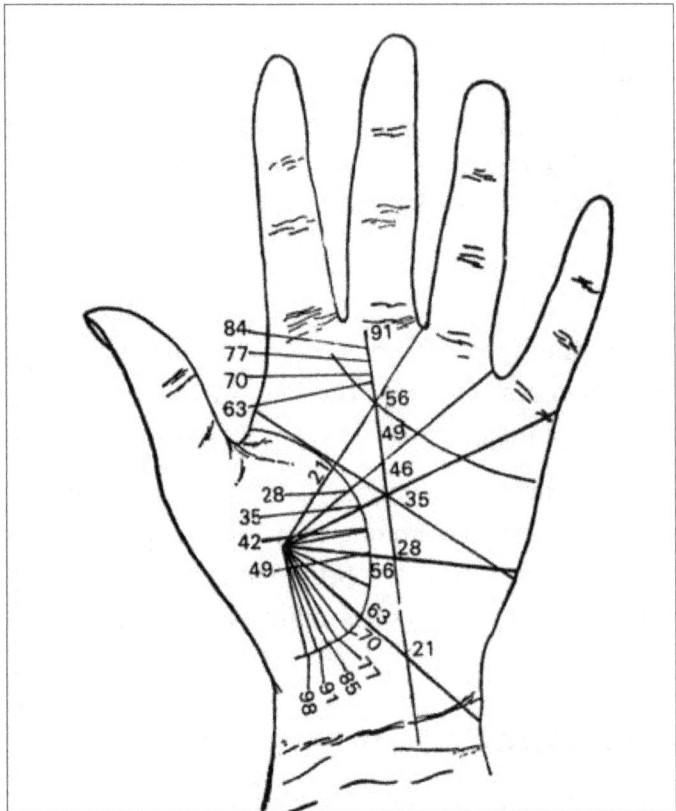

Figure 3.2. Gauging time on the hand.

Courtesy of Nitin Kumar.

- lack of clearly defined goals in life
- lack of courage
- tendency to scatter one's energies
- loss of wealth (especially when broken)
- loss of memory (especially when the strength of the lines is uneven)

Hindu palmists believe that the color of the lines have special meanings:

- Pink, clear, narrow lines: wealth
- Pale, whitish lines: poverty
- Reddish lines: strong personality; abundant energy
- Yellowish, golden lines: selfish, inhibited personality
- Brownish lines: spiteful, unforgiving nature

Atma Rekha (*Rohini*)

Atma rekha, which is also known variously as the "father line," *Gothra rehka*, *Puri rekha* and *Rohini* (Figure 3.1a) corresponds to the life line in Western palmistry.

However, instead of beginning above the thumb joint as the life line does, many Indian hand readers teach that it begins at the base of the hand near the wrist. (Note that palmist Nitin Kumar maintains that it begins at a point above the thumb joint).

In some cases, it starts at the *Mani-Bandha rekha*, or what Western palmists call the Rascettes of Venus (Figure 3.3).

Indian palmists believe, as many Western palmists do, that the individual is able to increase the length of this line by changes in attitude as well as lifestyle changes such as diet, exercise and stress management.

Like the life line of Western palmistry, Atma rekha is believed to indicate the potential length of life. Ideally, it should be slightly reddish in color, indicating good health and a strong physical constitution. Gaps, breaks, and islands can be signs of serious illness or accident.

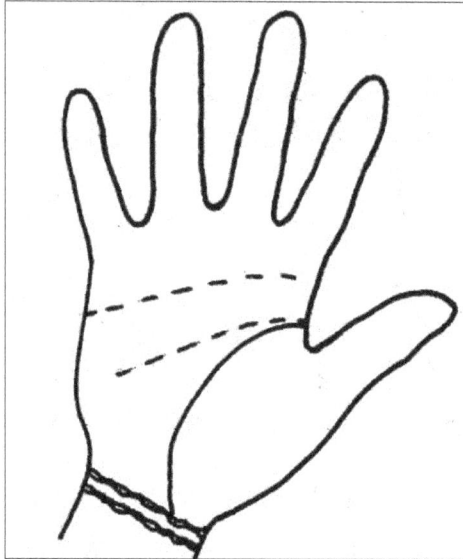

Figure 3.3. Atma rekha beginning at Mani-Bandha rekha.

If this line moves right into the base of the index finger (Figure 3.4), the person is said to be destined to live for at least a hundred years.

If this line contains a branch running up towards the *Pithru sthana* (Figure 3.5), the person will likely attain a high position in their chosen profession.

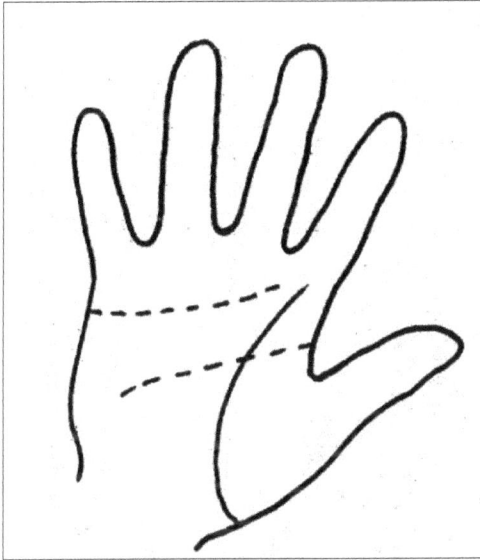

**Figure 3.4. Atma rekha "ending"
at the base of the index finger.**

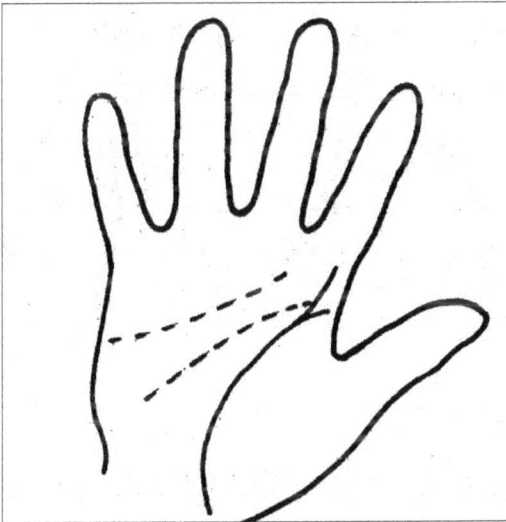

Figure 3.5. Branch from Atma rekha towards Pithru sthana.

If a small dot appears on this line, it foretells the birth of a son at the age where the dot appears. However, of the dot is black in color, the person will likely be involved in a scandal.

When found on a woman's hand, a small star formation at the end of this line indicates widowhood.

Bandha Rekha (*Aya Rehka*)

Bandha rekha (Figure 3.1b) corresponds to the heart line in Western palmistry. While in the West the line is said to begin at the percussion of the hand under the little finger and end between the middle and index finger, traditional Hindu palmists believe that this line ends under the *Jaya sthana*, which corresponds to the mount of Mercury in Western palmistry.

Although many modern Indian hand readers believe that the characteristics and meanings of this line are similar to those of the West, traditional Hindu palmists teach that it is more like a life line or a "line of character."

The Sanskrit term *bandha* has to do with the Hindu concept of bondage, or life on this earth. When this line begins at the base of the index finger, ends at the percussion of the hand, and is free from breaks or color changes, traditional Indian palmists believe that the person will live for a hundred years.

Because *Bandha rekha* moves across the top of the palm, it is believed to reflect the influences of several of the sthanas and thus affect the person's entire life. Generally speaking, the longer the line, the greater the potential for longevity.

Dhan Rekha (*Matri Rekha*)

The Western head line is called the *Dhan rekha, Matri rekha* or "mother line" by the Hindus (Figure 3.1c). Like the head line, the Dhan rekha reflects the mental processes, including reasoning ability, imagination, self-control, and clarity of mind.

Among the early Hindus, it was believed that the length and clarity of this line revealed one's potential wealth and material possessions, because the careful use of intelligence and reasoning powers would naturally lead to power, position and economic abundance.

If this line is connected to the Atma rekha (Figure 3.6), Indian palmists consider it a sign of good fortune in that the person is likely to accumulate much property during their life.

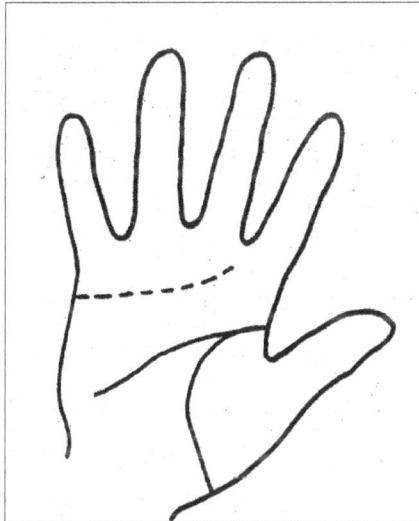

Figure 3.6. Dhan rekha connected to the Atma rekha.

Indira Rekha

Named for Indira, the Hindu Goddess of Wealth, this line (Figure 3.1d) corresponds to both the destiny (or fate) line in Western palmistry and the *Column of Jade* of the Chinese palmistry school.

The longer, deeper, and clearer the line, the greater the chances of achieving career success and enjoying material abundance throughout life. According to tradition, you need to read this line on the right hand of males and on the left hand of females.

Ideally, this line should begin at the base of the palm (just above the *Mani Banda rekha*) and be long. clear and straight, ending at or above the joint of the middle finger. Breaks in this line indicate financial reversals and crises in one's professional life. Traditionally, it was believed that a broken Indira rekha on the hand of a woman indicated that she would become a widow.

If this line begins within what Westerners call the mount of Luna (Figure 3.7) it means that the person's career depends largely on the decisions and caprices of others rather than on one's efforts alone.

If this line begins within the Atma rekha or life line (Figure 3.8), the career is dependent on the family's influence, especially its social or economic status. A young person who would join the family business or be hired by a company due to a parent's influence or social position, would likely have such a line in their hand.

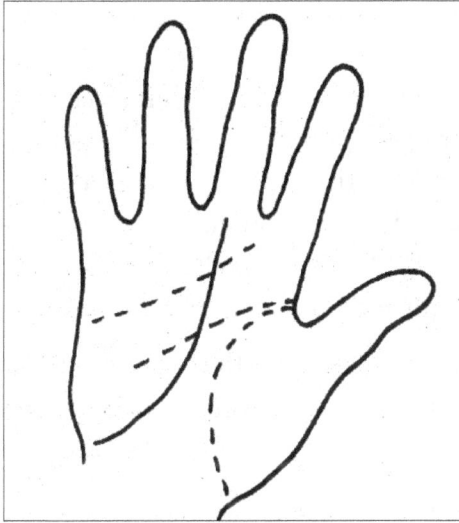

Figure 3.7. Indira rekha beginning on mount of Luna.

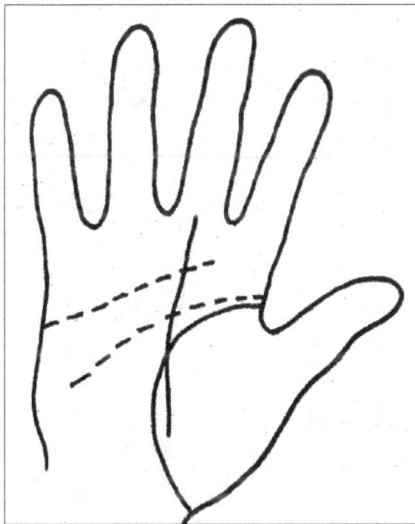

Figure 3.8. Indira rekha beginning within Atma rekha.

Kamala Rekha / Vidya Rekha

Often accompanying a strong Indira rekha, the *Kamala rekha* (Figure 3.1e) corresponds to the Apollo line in the Western palmistry tradition. This line usually begins just above the Bandha rekha and ends at a point just below the ring finger. When it is long, clear and strong, it indicates long life, wealth and the potential for renown.

If this line moves from the base of the palm well into the second or middle phalange or the ring finger (Figure 3.9), it is called the *Vidya rekha* or the "line of learning."

Considered a highly favorable line to have, the presence of this rare *rekha* indicates that the person will likely achieve a high degree of accomplishment in the arts and sciences. It can also indicate fame as a writer, professor or scientist.

And like the more common Kamala rekha described earlier, it also foretells the potential for a long and prosperous life.

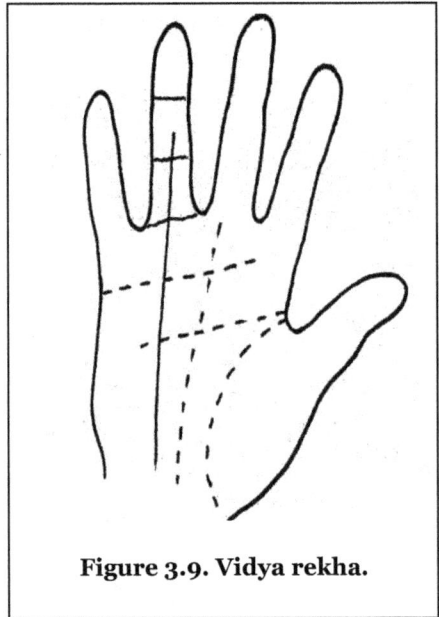

Figure 3.9. Vidya rekha.

44

Bala Rekha

The location of the *Bala rekha* (Figure 3.1f) corresponds to the Mercury or stomach line in Western palmistry. When clear, long, free from breaks and slightly golden in color, Indian palmists believe that it is a sign that the person will enjoy long life and maintain a youthful appearance even in old age.

Mandoshnada Rekha

The meaning of this line (Figure 3.1g), which can be equated to the Girdle of Venus of Western palmistry, is often a subject of controversy among Indian palmists. Students of the Kartikeyan system believe that this line reveals a cold heart and a dull intellect, with its owner having poor career possibilities in life.

Other palmists claim that when this line is clear, well-formed and pinkish in color, it reveals an individual with high literary taste and strong abilities as a writer.

However, if the line is broken, poorly-formed and pale in color, the person would tend to be greedy and selfish.

If the *Mandoshnada rekha* is short and runs from the base of the middle finger to the base of the little finger (as seen in Figure 3.10) Indian palmists believe that the person will likely be a liar and a cheat.

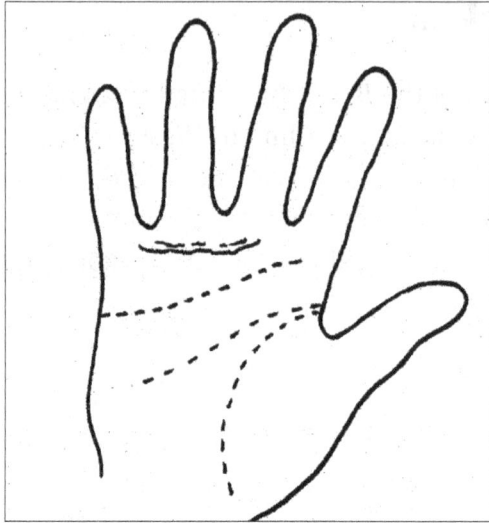

Figure 3.10. Mandoshnada rekha (short).

4. The Minor Lines

In addition to the seven major rekhas of the hand, there are more than twenty minor rekhas and other markings that play an important role in Hindu palmistry.

Mani-Bandha Rekha

While similar in appearance to the Rascettes of Venus in Western palmistry, *Mani-Bandha rekha* (also known as *Yav mala*) has a variety of meanings unique to Indian tradition.

- One bracelet with several islands (Figure 4.1): a life of poverty and economic struggle

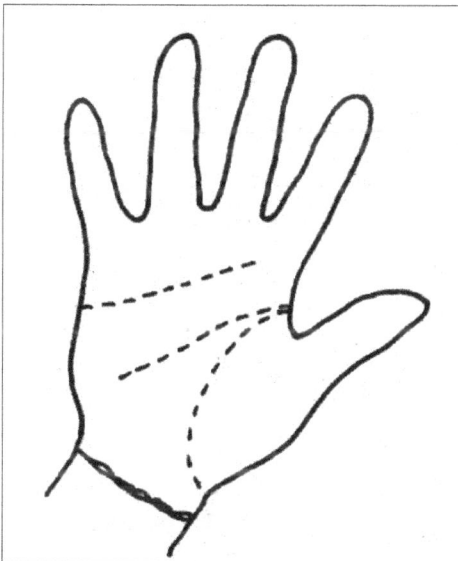

Figure 4.1. One bracelet with several islands.

- Two bracelets containing several islands each: a reasonably happy life, with adequate income
- Three bracelets with several islands each (Figure 4.2) a life of happiness and wealth

- If two bracelets go completely around the wrist: great wealth and wisdom

- If three bracelets go completely around the wrist: an exalted position in life, with great wealth, power, and influence. However, if the lines are badly chained, life will be difficult. Eventual success, however, is assured through intense personal effort.

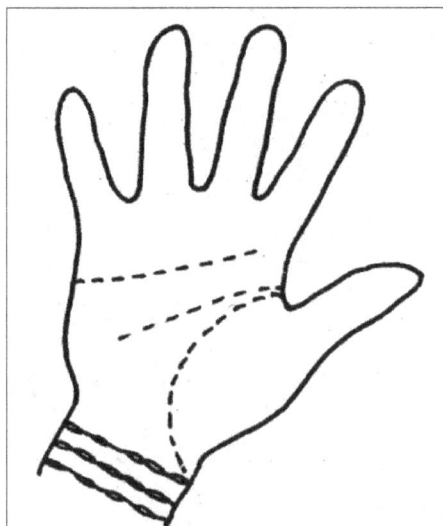

Figure 4.2. Three bracelets with several islands.

Pasa Rekha

This formation has no corresponding line in Western palmistry. Although rarely found in its pure state, the *Pasa rekha* is formed by an oval that appears in the center of the palm (Figure 4.3). It is a sign that the person will be able to overcome all of life's obstacles.

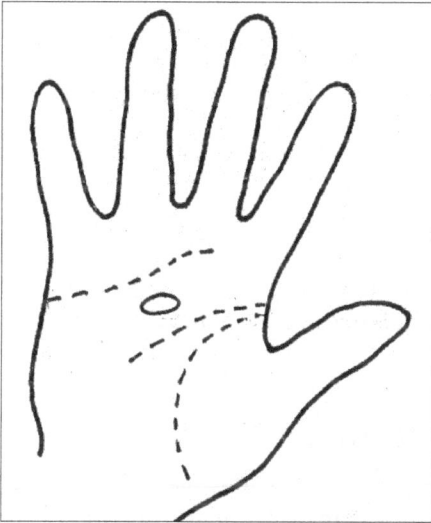

Figure 4.3. Pasa rekha

Kamahastika Rekha

A small line beginning above the Bandha rekha and moving towards the middle finger (Figure 4.4), the *Kamahastika rekha* often runs parallel to the Indira rekha or destiny line. Whenever it appears, it is a sign of good fortune. When found on a man's hand, it foretells happiness from his children; if found on a woman's hand, she will enjoy abundant wealth and overall good fortune.

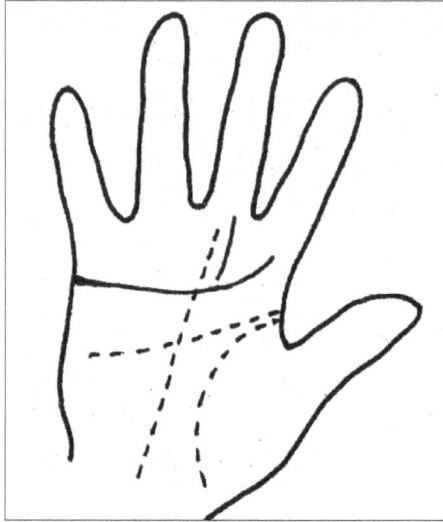

Figure 4.4. Kamahastika rekha.

Korpara Rekha

Considered important only if found on the left hand, this sign consists of three, four or five parallel vertical lines that form a cluster under the ring finger (Figure 4.5). Their presence indicates frequent travel.

Dharani Rekha

Consisting of a vertical line rising just above the joint at the base of the index finger (Figure 4.6), the *Dharani rekha* favors the accumulation of large real estate holdings.

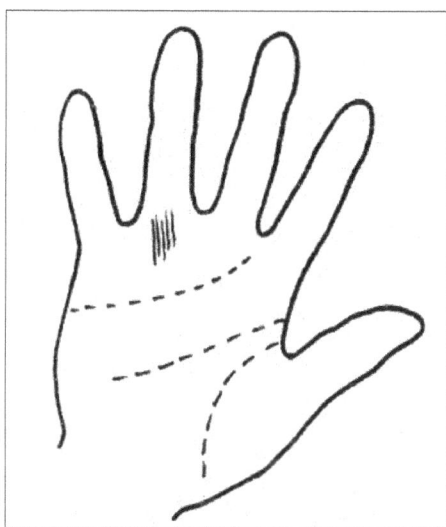

Figure 4.5. Korpara rekha.

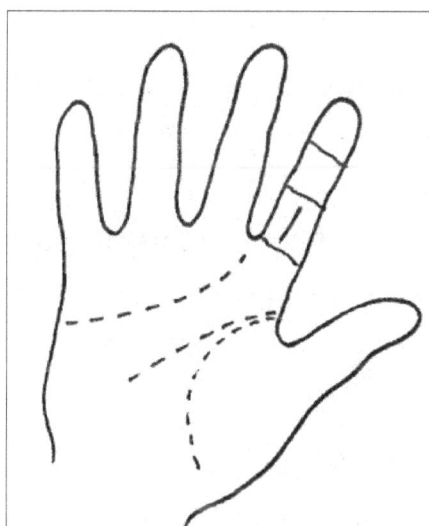

Figure 4.6. Dharani rekha.

Hemavalli Rekha

The presence of this small line reaching to the ring finger (Figure 4.7) is considered quite favorable by teachers of the Kartikeyan school of palmistry, because it is a sign that the person will enjoy sexual pleasure from youth through old age.

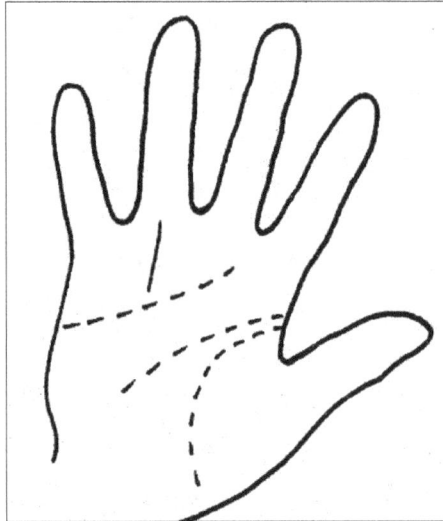

Figure 4.7. Hemavalli rekha.

Varistha Rekha

Consisting of several strong vertical lines on the base phalange of the index finger (Figure 4.8), *Varistha rekha* has to do with one's extended family. It not only indicates that the person has many aunts, uncles or cousins, but that relatives will help the individual attain their goals in life.

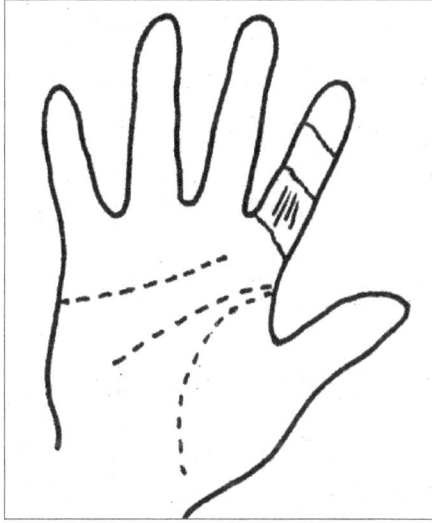

Figure 4.8. Varistha rekha.

Diksha Rekha

Similar in form to the Ring of Solomon of Western palmistry, this small line moves diagonally across the Pithru sthana under the index finger (Figure 4.9). Known also as the "line of renunciation," it is found primarily on the hands of people who lead a life of sacrifice and selfless service to others.

Hara Rekha

This line forms a small ring around the base of the middle finger (Figure 4.10), Traditionally, the presence of *hara* was a sign of good fortune, due to its purported connection to royalty. If found on a man's hand, it would make him "beloved by his king"; today, it would mean that he would be a protégé of a high-ranking public official, popular entertainer, or company president.

If *hara* appeared on a woman's hand, it indicated that she would be favored as a royal consort or concubine. Like contemporary males, such women today would more likely become associated with an important leader in entertainment, business or politics, and not necessarily as a sexual partner.

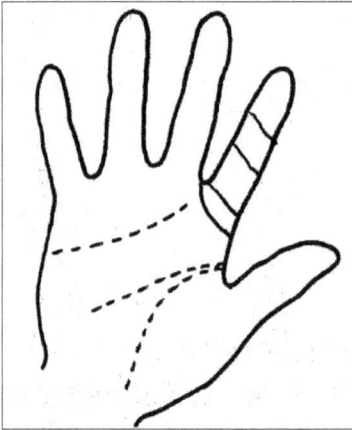

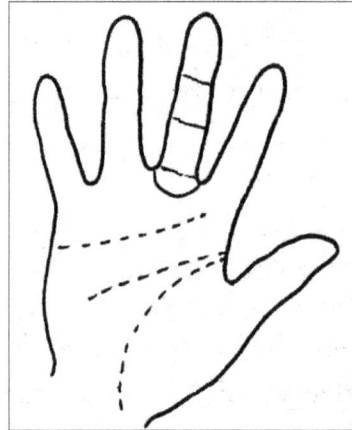

Figure 4.9. Diksha rekha.   Figure 4.10. Hara rekha.

The Triangle of Mars

The *Triangle of Mars* is formed by the Atma rekha, Dhan rekha and Bala rekha (Figure 4.11). When it is well-marked, distinct and unbroken, this triangle is considered to favor a prosperous, healthy and long life. However, if the angles formed by these lines are unusually wide or narrow, some specific interpretations apply:

- If angle "a" is wide: sign of a tenderhearted person
- If angle "a" is narrow: person tends to be foolish or impolite
- If angle "b" is wide: long life; good memory; the person is mischievous and easily excited
- If angle" b" is narrow: person is restless and unsettled in life
- If angle "c" is wide: healthy; honest
- If angle "c" is narrow: greedy; weak intellect

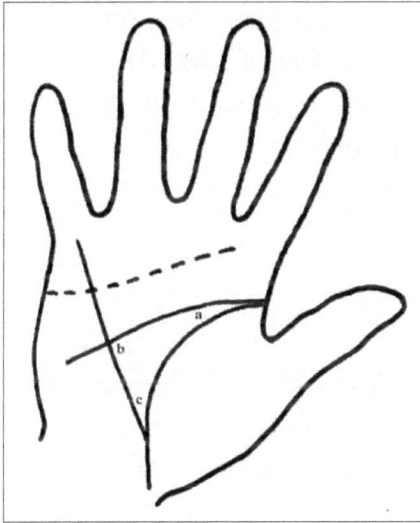

Figure 4.11. The Triangle of Mars.

The Quadrangle

The *Quadrangle* is formed by the Dhan rekha, Bandha rekha, Indira rekha and Bala rekha (Figure 4.12). Like the

Triangle of Mars, the appearance of the Quadrangle has different interpretations in Indian palmistry.

- If broad and squarish: person is highly principled and loyal
- If the space between Dhan rekha and Bandha rekha is wide: person tends to be trustworthy
- If the space between Dhan rekha and Bandha rekha is narrow: person tends to be malicious, greedy and deceitful
- If the space closest to Dharma rekha is narrower than the space under Vidya sthana: person tends to be greedy and closed-minded
- If the Indira rekha and the Bala rekha are indistinct: person tends to be secretive and greedy

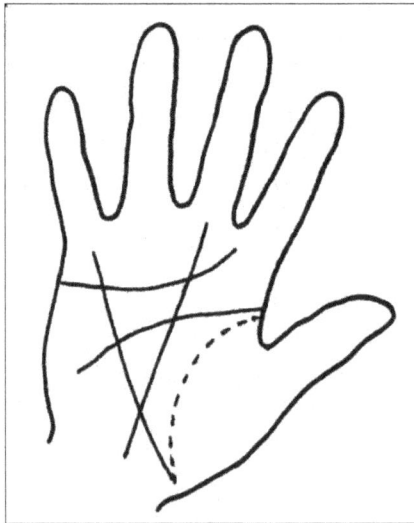

Figure 4.12. The Quadrangle.

Mahi Rekha

Mahi rekha (Figure 4.13) consists of a clear and unbroken line (i.e. one that is not crossed or broken by any other line), moving slightly downwards from the edge of the Jaya sthana, or mount of Mercury.

Long considered a favorable sign, it reveals that its owner is destined to learn the meaning of all the Shastras, or the Hindu texts of Divine Law. If found on the hand of a non-Hindu, it would conceivably mean that the person would likely become an expert in their chosen religious or philosophical field: a noted Biblical scholar, a teacher of the Kabbalah or an authority on existentialism or on the Holy Koran.

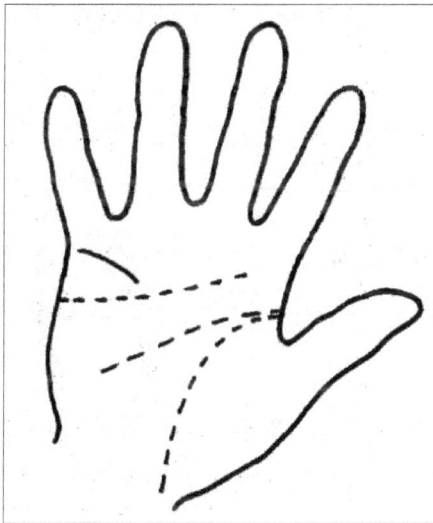

Figure 4.13. Mahi Rekha.

Jaya Rekha

Also known as *hridgata-hatwada*, these small lines are similar to the union lines in Western palmistry, and represent marriage-quality relationships (Figure 14.4). Branches at the end of a *Jaya rekha* indicate separation. If the line droops towards the Bandha rekha (Figure 4.15), it is a sign that the person's partner will die first.

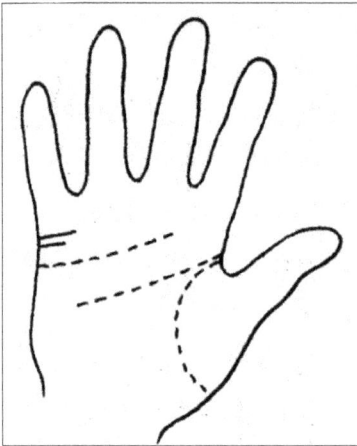

Figure 4.14. Jaya Rekha.

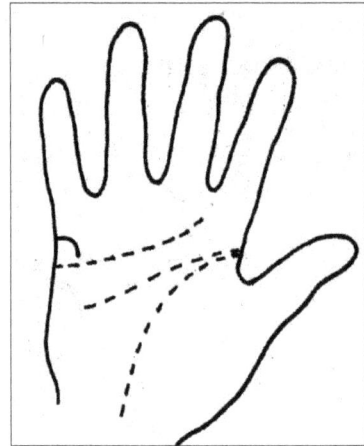

Figure 4.15. Jaya rekha drooping towards Bandha rekha.

Lines Depicting Brothers and Sisters

A number of lines, known as *Kanishthra rekha*, are similar in form to the influence lines of the Western palmistry tradition. Beginning below the thumb and moving across the end of the Atma rekha and towards the index finger (Figure 4.16), each line is believed to indicate a brother or sister; the deeper lines represent brothers, while the thinner lines indicate sisters.

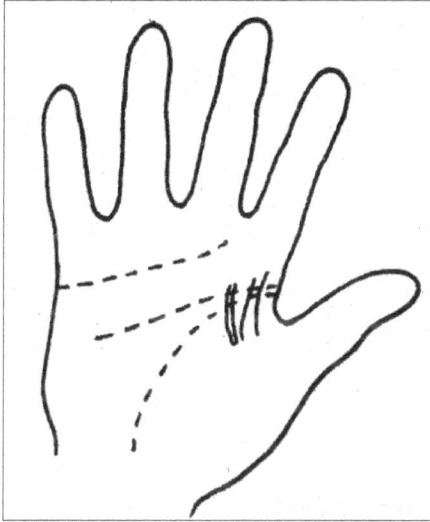

Figure 4.16. Lines indicating siblings.

Other palmists teach that small horizontal lines, located at the percussion of the right hand between the Bandha rekha and Dhan rekha (Figure 4. 17) indicate the number of brothers one has (or is likely to have).

Sister lines are located on the percussion of the right hand in the region of the Lunar mount in Western palmistry (Figure 4.18).

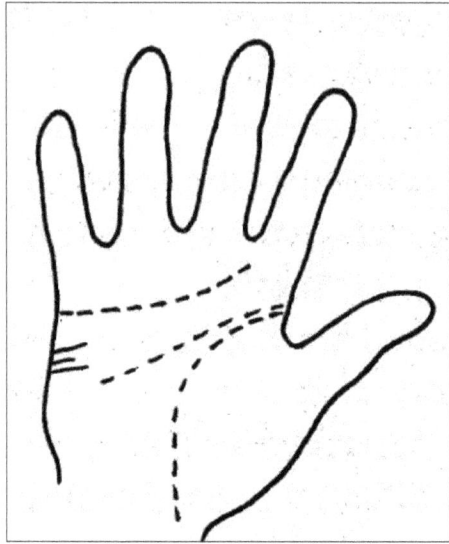

Figure 4.17. Lines indicating brothers.

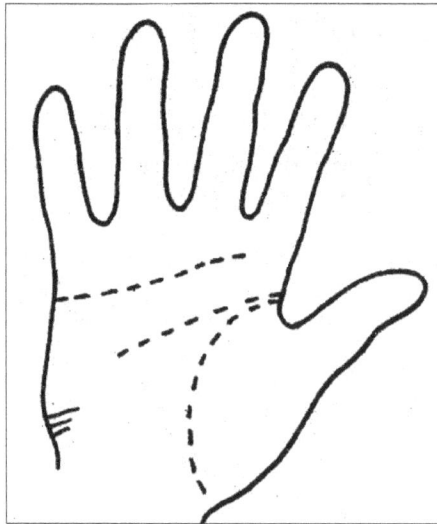

Figure 4.18. Lines indicating sisters.

Lines Indicating Children

Children have always been considered extremely important in India, and although family planning has begun to limit their size, Indians traditionally have had large families. In a country where the extended family is the most important social unit, couples who do not have children are considered a failure or even a disgrace. For these reasons, it is not surprising that there are several methods for reading children in a person's hand.

In Hindu palmistry, it is believed that small lines on the Sathru sthana, running parallel to the Atma rekha or life line, indicate the number of children one will have (Figure 4.19).

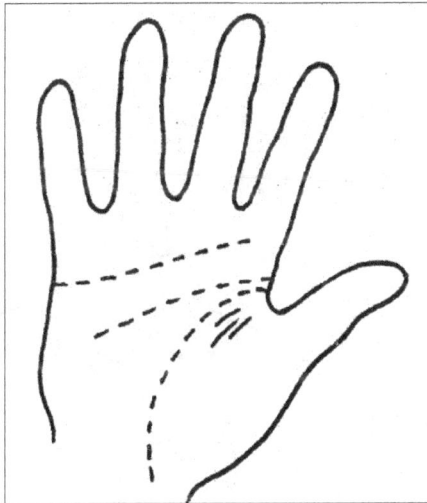

Figure 4.19. Lines indicating three children.

When found on the Putra Sankhya sthana or the Putra sthana (Figure 4.20), it is believed to indicate the number of children one will have.

Children lines can also be seen at the base of the palm, running parallel to the lower joint of the thumb. A thick and long line is supposed to indicate a son, while a thin and short line would likely reveal a daughter.

Figure 4.21 shows that the person will likely be the parent of three daughters and one son. If the line is very short and weak, the child will likely be sickly or can die at an early age.

Islands found in the lower thumb joint of the right hand (Figure 4.22) are believed to indicate children as well: each island is said to represent a son or daughter.

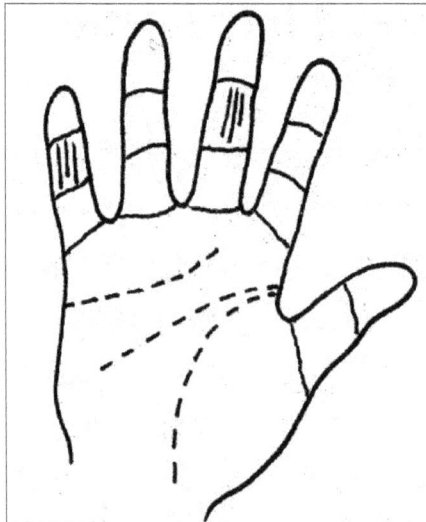

Figure 4.20. Lines indicating six children.

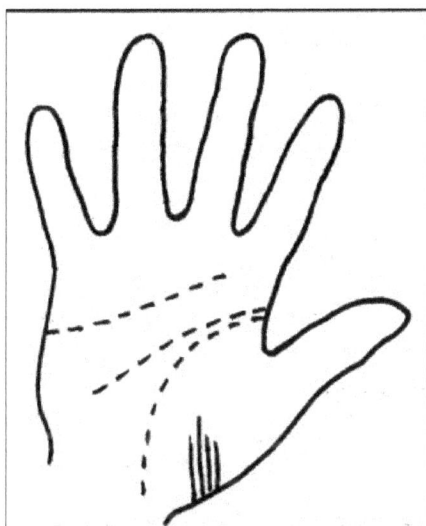

**Figure 4.21. Lines indicating
three daughters and one son.**

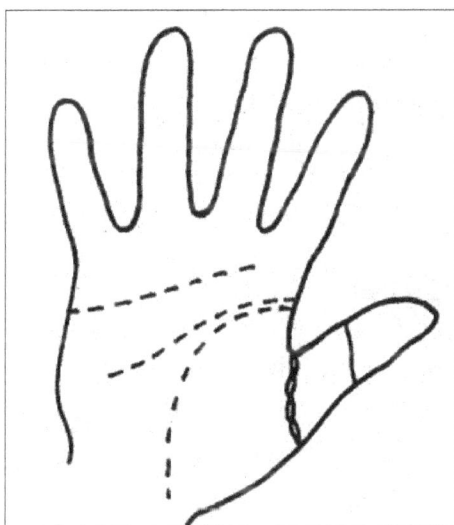

Figure 4.22. Islands indicating four children.

Other Lines on the Fingers

Indian palmists take great care in examining any small or thin lines that appear on the fingers. While they may not be the most important lines on the hand, they are believed to reveal important trends in a person's life and can substantially alter the significance of other lines and markings. Some lines on the fingers have already been discussed. Here are others that are important:

Index Finger

- A line beginning at the base of the index finger and ending on the second *parva* or phalange (Figure 4.23): a thoughtful and wise person; strong sense of pride
- Horizontal lines across top phalange: inheritance
- Small vertical lines on middle phalange (Figure 4.24): many children
- Small vertical lines on third (base) phalange: jovial disposition

Middle Finger

- Several long vertical lines moving up the entire middle finger (Fig. 4.25): success in mining
- Several vertical lines on the top phalange (Fig. 4.26): acquisitive and greedy
- Several vertical lines on the base phalange (Fig.4.27): misfortune

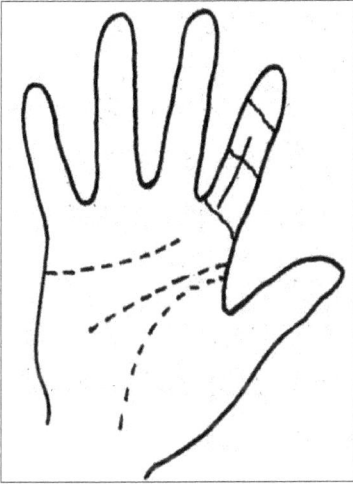

Figure 4.23. Line ending in second phalange of index finger.

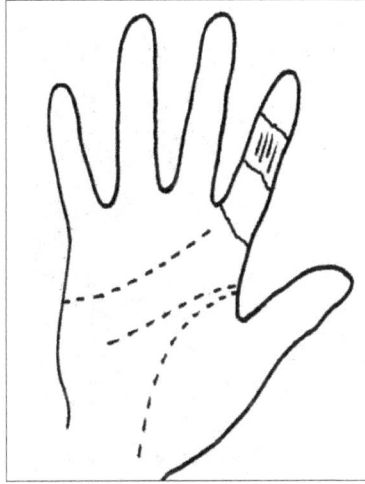

Figure 4.24. Small vertical lines in second phalange of index finger.

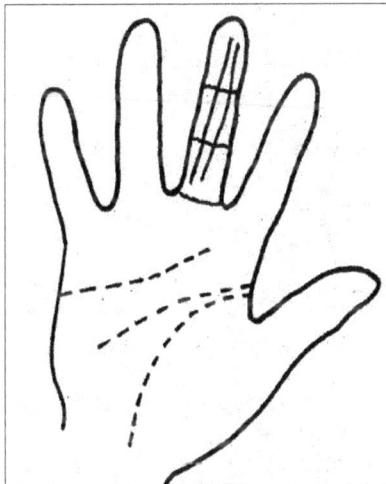

Figure 4.25. Vertical lines on the middle Finger.

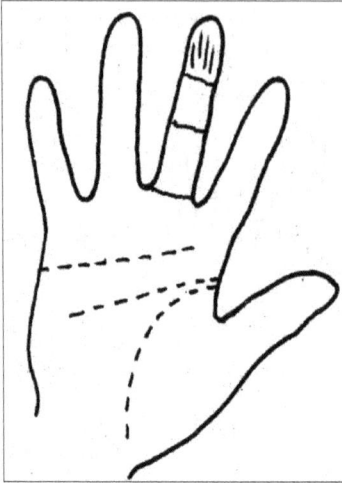

Figure 4.26. Vertical lines on the top phalange of middle finger.

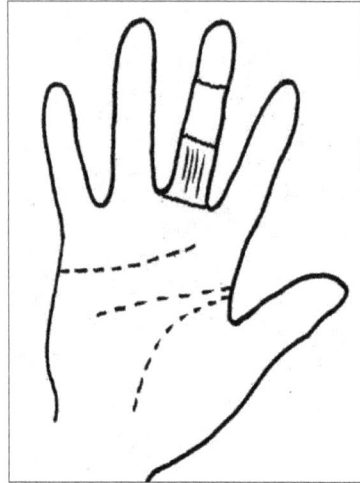

Figure 4.27. Vertical lines on the base phalange of middle finger.

Ring Finger

- One straight vertical line from the base to the top phalange (Figure 4.28): great good fortune
- Two or more straight vertical lines from the base to the top phalange: will lose money due to illicit romantic affairs
- One straight vertical line from the base phalange to the middle phalange: person is extravagant with money
- Several small vertical lines on middle phalange: fame

Little Finger

- One straight line from the base to the top phalange: mark of strong spirituality; sign of a deep thinker and scholar, especially in philosophy or religion
- Deep line on the top phalange (Figure 4.29): delicate health

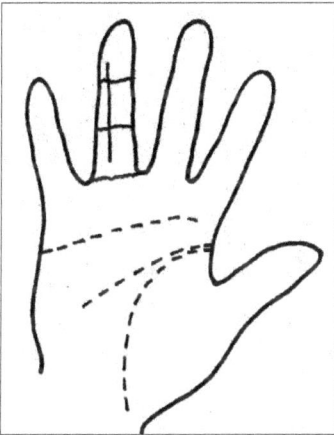

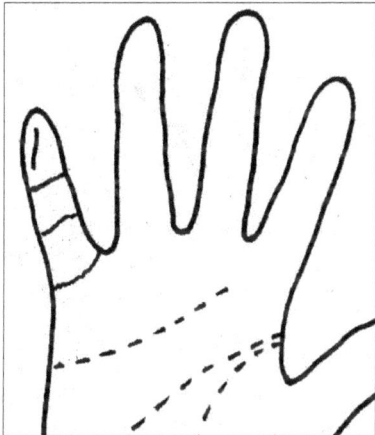

Figure 4.28. One straight line from third to first phalange of ring finger.

Figure 4.29. One deep line on first phalange of little finger.

- Two or more straight vertical lines on the second (middle) phalange (Figure 4.30): proficiency in the occult sciences, such as astrology, palmistry, tarot or esoteric healing.
- Cross bars on the middle phalange (Figure 4. 31): sign of a thief or deceitful person
- Line from the *Jaya sthana* to middle phalange (Figure 4.32): sign of a "self-made" woman or man

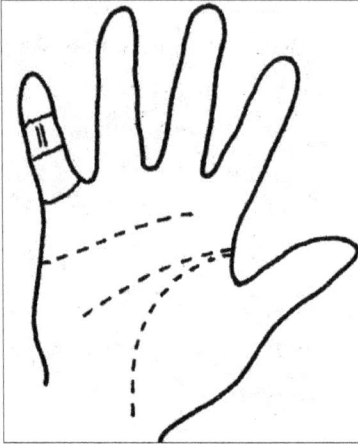

Figure 4:30. Two vertical lines on second phalange of little finger.

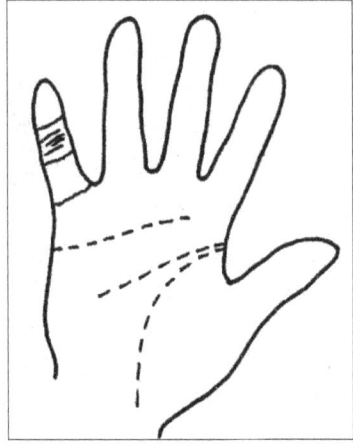

Figure 4.31. Cross bars on middle phalange of little finger.

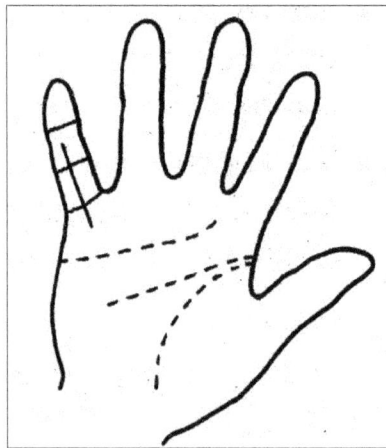

Figure 4.32. Line from Jaya sthana into second phalange of little finger.

The Thumb

- Four horizontal lines on second (lower) phalange (Figure 4.33): fame and wealth
- Two or more lines from the Brathru sthana moving into first (top) phalange (Figure 4.34): the person is ardent and sincere in love
- Two or more lines moving from the Brathru sthana into the second (lower) phalange: person is the object of universal affection among friends, family and acquaintances

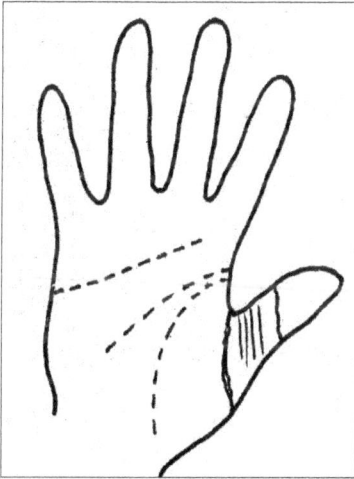

Figure 4.33. Four horizontal lines on lower phalange of the thumb.

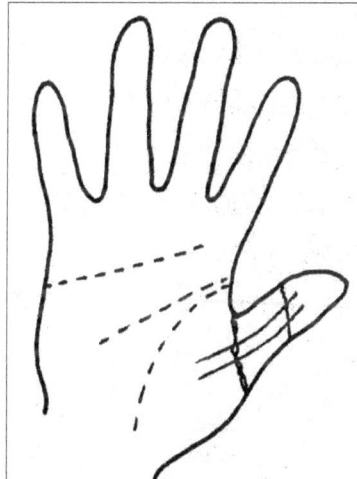

Figure 4.34. Lines from Brathru sthana into top phalange of the thumb.

5. Signs and Symbols

Indian palmistry teaches that specialized signs and symbols are found throughout the palm and fingers. Some of them have specific meanings, while others reveal a general quality, such as "good fortune" or "happy marriage." Several signs are extremely rare and found only on the hands of saints and other extraordinary individuals. Since there are literally hundreds of specialized markings, we will cover only some of the most common ones here.

The Canopy

Considered a rare sign, the *Canopy* (Figure 5.1) is a symbol of high spiritual and moral attainment wherever it appears on the palm. It is sometimes found on the hands of yogis and *saddhus*, but can appear on those of learned scholars, writers and teachers as well.

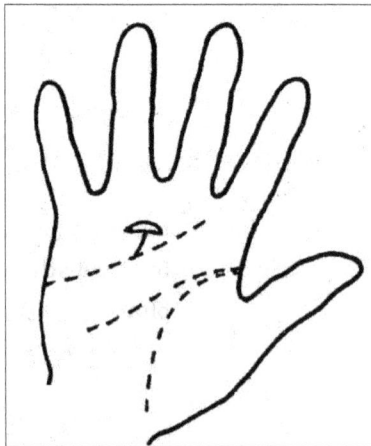

Figure 5.1. The Canopy

The Circle

In Hindu palmistry some practitioners believe that a *circle* is significant only when found on the top phalange (*parva*) of the fingers and thumb.

It is believed that these tiny circles (only slightly larger than a dot) tend to cluster in groups of up to ten, and have the following (and sometimes curious) meanings:

- One circle: the person is clever
- Two circles (Figure 5.2): physical attractiveness

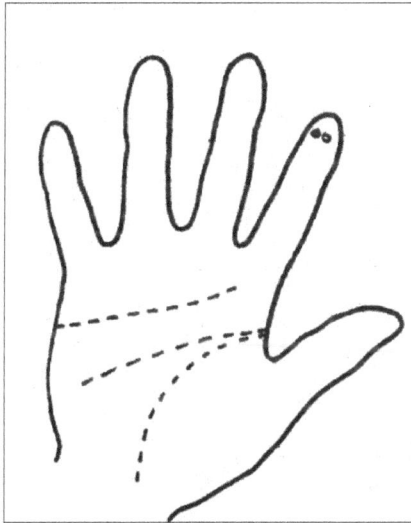

Figure 5.2. Two tiny circles.

- Three circles: the individual is (or will likely be) wealthy
- Four circles: the person is (or is likely to be) poor
- Five circles (Figure 5.3): well-educated
- Six circles: intelligence

- Seven circles: the person will lead a solitary life
- Eight circles: the person is (or will be) poor
- Nine circles: the individual will be distinguished as a government leader
- Ten circles: the person will be employed as a civil servant

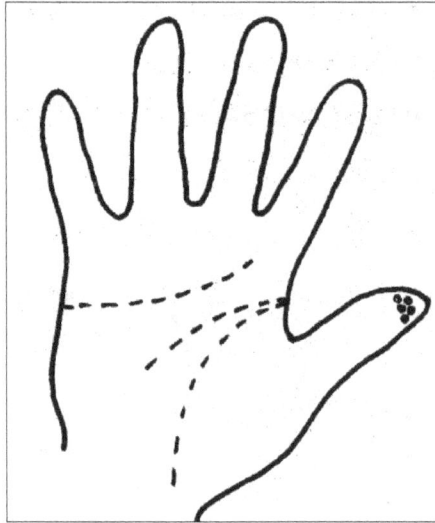

Figure 5.3. Five tiny circles.

Some Indian palmists maintain that the presence of a larger single circle or oval will sometimes have special significance, depending on where it is found on the palm and fingers.

- When found under the ring finger (Figure 5.4): fame and wealth
- When located on the mount of Luna: danger and death by drowning

- When a single circle is found anywhere else on the hand or fingers: misfortune

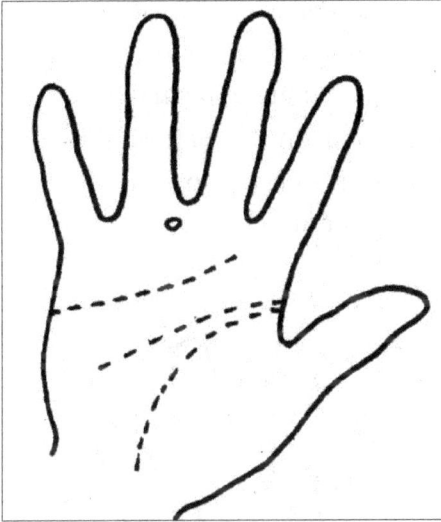

Figure 5.4. Circle under the ring finger.

The Cross

The *Cross* is composed of two small yet distinct lines that are not part of any other line. It is generally considered an unfavorable sign to have, with two exceptions:

- When located on the Pithru sthana: happy marriage
- When found on the Vidya sthana: person will achieve fame and wealth
- When appearing on the Mathru sthana and touching the Indira rekha: sign of possible accident and premature death

- When found on the Jaya sthana: the person is a liar and a thief
- When found on the Dharma sthana: sign of an obstinate and quarrelsome nature
- When found on either the Brathru sthana or Bandhu sthana: unhappy marriage
- When located on the Sathru sthana (Figure 5.5.): the individual is likely to suffer injury or death due to a quarrel or attack

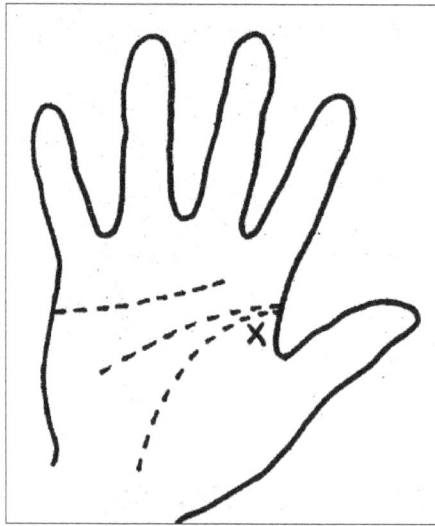

Figure 5.5. Cross on the Satru sthana.

- When found on the Lunar mount: danger of death by drowning
- When located at a point just above the Bandha rekha (Figure 5.6): danger of severe head injury
- When appearing on the third (or base) phalange of the middle finger (on a female hand): no children

- When appearing on the first (or top) phalange of the little finger: poverty; life without a mate

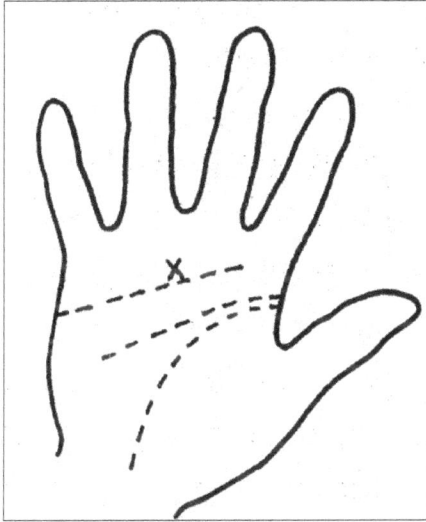

Figure 5.6. Cross above Bandha rekha.

Dots

As in Western palmistry, *dots* are usually an indicator of illness or accident.

A reddish dot appearing on the Bandha rekha (Figure 5.7) would indicate a possible accident or injury involving the head; a yellowish dot on the Atma rekha would be a sign of liver disease at the approximate age where it appears on the line.

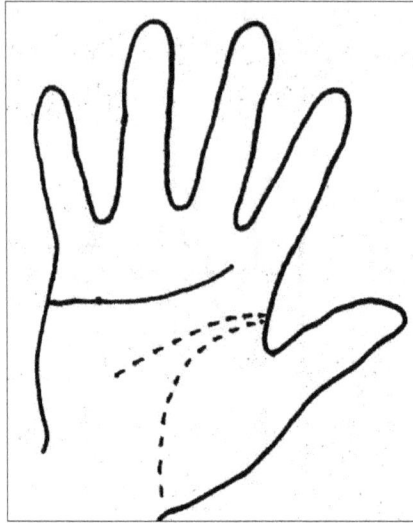

Figure 5.7. A dot on Bandha rekha.

A dot appearing at the end of a line would reveal a sudden and catastrophic end to the qualities that the line represents. If found at the end of the Indira rekha, for example, the profession might end in disaster or the person might lose his or her wealth. If appearing at the end of a marriage line, the marriage would end suddenly due to death or scandal.

The Fish

This curious symbol is found above the wrist (Figure 5.8). Its presence on the hand reveals prosperity and good fortune. The *Fish* is sometimes found on the hand of a person who is likely to have a major leadership role in their community, and who is known for benevolence and charity towards others.

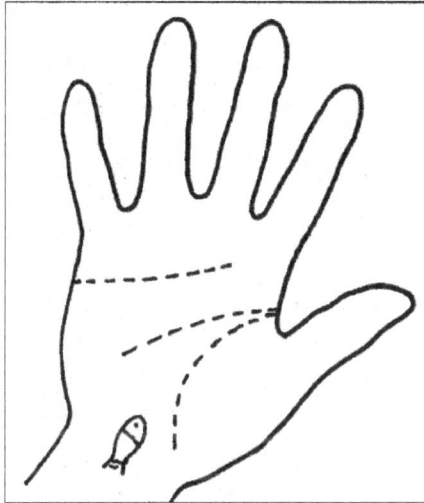

Figure 5.8. The Fish.

The Flag

The presence of this rare marking (Figure 5.9) anywhere

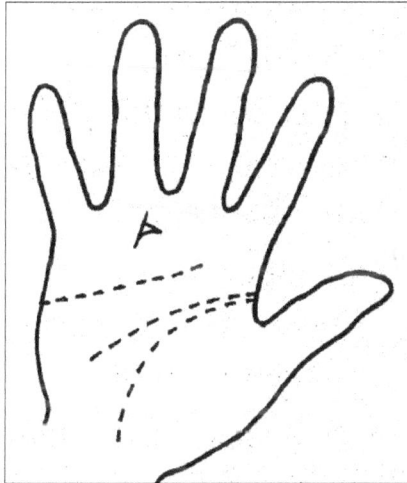

Figure 5.9. The Flag.

on the palm is considered a sign of moral courage and purity of character The *Flag* is sometimes found on the hands of wealthy and influential individuals who are admired and respected in their community.

The Grille

As in the West, the *grille* is considered an unfortunate sign in traditional Indian palmistry. Its presence tends to diminish the positive qualities of the *sthana* on which it appears.

- If located on the Pithru sthana (Figure 5.10): the owner tends to be egotistical, domineering and stubborn
- If found on the Mathru sthana: prone to depression and melancholy
- A grille on the Vidya sthana: sign of a superstitious nature
- If appearing on the Jaya sthana: the person cannot be trusted
- A grille on the Dharma sthana: sign of a sudden, premature death
- If appearing on the mount of Luna: suicidal tendencies

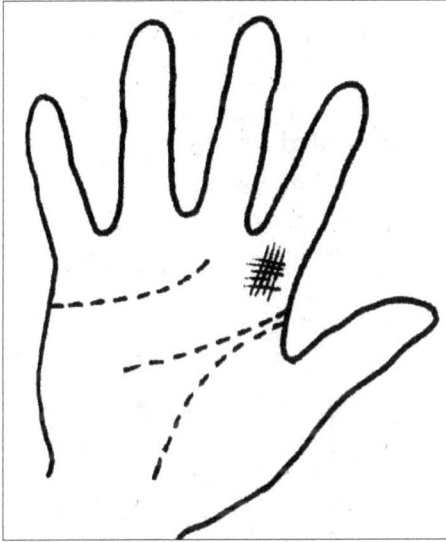

Figure 5.10. Grille on Pithru sthana.

Islands

Islands are also considered unfortunate in Hindu palmistry, because they usually* indicate periods of weakness or misfortune wherever it appears on a line.

- An island on the Jaya rekha (marriage line) for example (Figure 5.11): major problems in the person's primary relationship
- Islands on the Indira rekha: serious reversals in career or finances; loss of wealth through sexual intrigue

*with the exception of indicating the number of children, described on page 62

- Islands on the Bandha rekha: adulterous affairs; if the Pithru sthana is large and fleshy as well: heart disease
- An island located at the end of a line: the person will end his or her days in misery

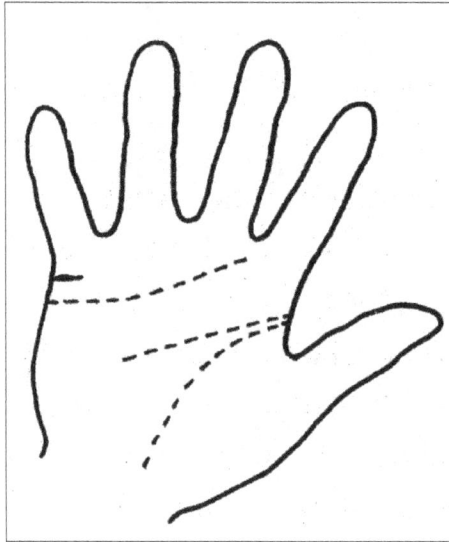

Figure 5.11. Island on Jaya rekha.

The Moon

The *Moon* (Figure 5.12) is a sign of a kind individual with a gentle disposition wherever it is found on the palm. Hindu palmists teach that those with this rare mark are loved and admired by large numbers of people.

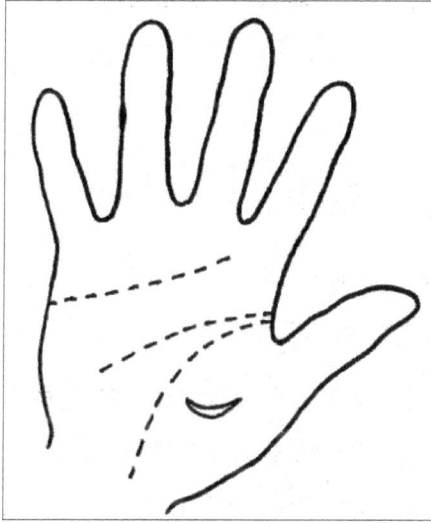

Figure 5.12. The Moon.

The Square

As in other palmistry schools, the Hindus teach that the *square* is a sign of protection and preservation that tends to cancel out the negative connotations of any broken or split lines in the hand.

If covering a break in the Indira rekha, for example (Figure 5.13) a square would save its owner from a severe business reversal or other career setback.

- A square appearing on Brathru sthana (Figure 5.14): person would likely be an authority in religion or philosophy
- A star within a square on Mathru sthana (Figure 5.15): protection from murder

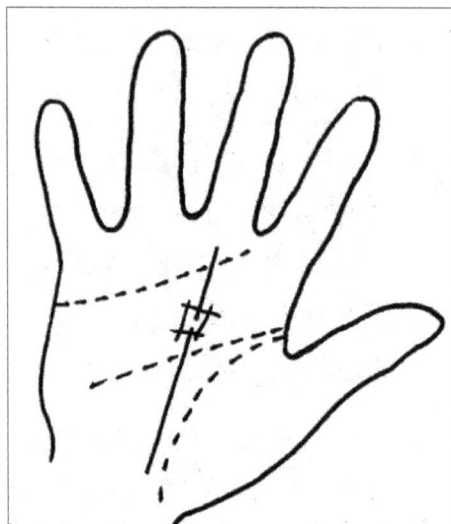

**Figure 5.13. Square covering
a break on a line.**

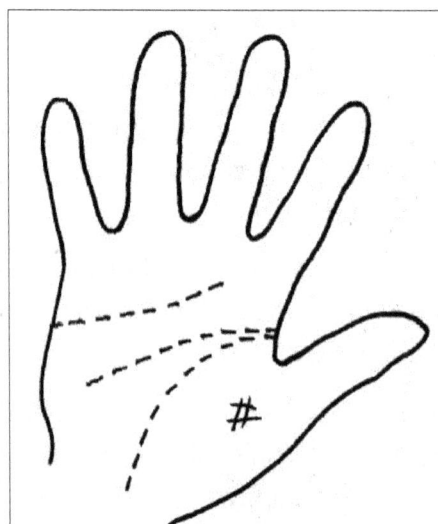

Figure 5.14. Square on Brathru sthana.

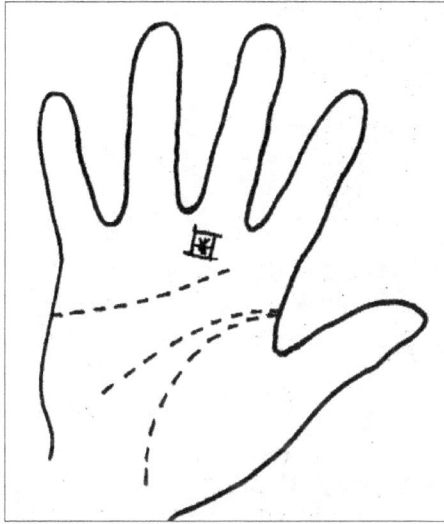

Figure 5.15. A star within a square.

The Star

The *Star* is made up of either three or six tiny lines forming a star-like pattern. Though usually considered a favorable sign, its meaning varies according to its clarity and its location on the hand. Generally speaking, a star is believed to indicate a situation that one cannot easily change.

- When a star is found at the end of the Atma rekha (Figure 5.16): person will achieve greatness due to his or her intellectual abilities.
- When located on the Atma rekha itself: danger of accident at the age where the star appears
- When found on the Mathru sthana on a hand with strong, clear lines (Figure 5.17): high attainment in life

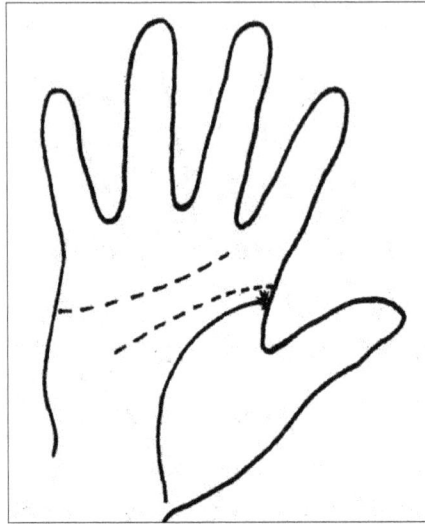

Figure 5.16. Star at the end of Atma rekha.

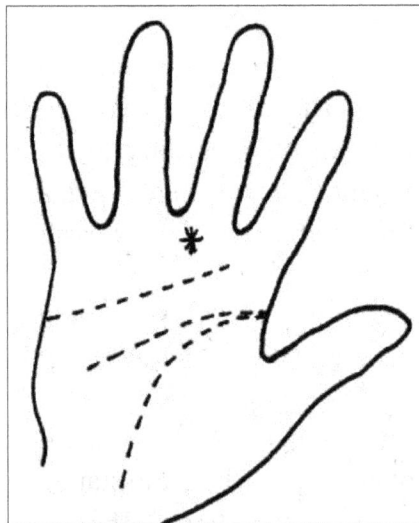

Figure 5.17. Star on Mathru sthana.

- When found on the Mathru sthana on a hand with poor lines: violent temper; homicidal tendencies
- When located on the Vidya sthana: great wealth, fame; excellent reputation
- When found on the Jaya sthana: untrustworthy; thief
- When found on the Dharma sthana: fame and accomplishment due to one's own tenacity. If found on both hands: suicidal tendencies
- When located on the Brathru sthana: major conquests in love and relationships
- When found in the center of the palm: sign of premature death surrounded by great publicity

The Sword

Also known as the *Kuthar rekha*, the *Sword* (Figure 5.18) has significance only when found on the Vidya sthana.

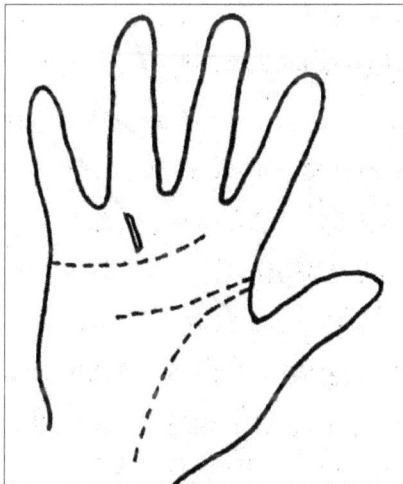

Figure 5.18. The Sword

85

Considered an unlucky sign, its presence indicates that the person's life will be one of challenge and struggle.

The Temple

A rare marking, the *Temple* (Figure 5.19) is occasionally found on the hands of people occupying a very high position in society, such as a multi-millionaire, a famous celebrity or a member of royalty.

Also found among noted scholars, religious leaders and accomplished writers, it is considered a sign that the individual will reach the heights of their profession or station in life.

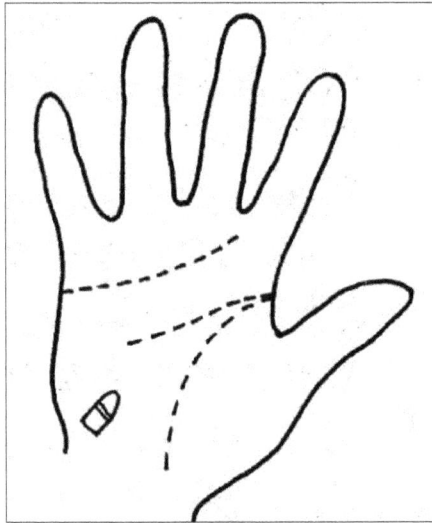

Figure 5.19. The Temple

The Tree

The *Tree* is often formed at the end of another line (Figure 5.20), though it can also involve the small lines that emanate upwards from a major line (Figure 5.21).

The presence of a tree is considered very positive by Hindu palmists, especially when it is found at the end of Indira rekha, Atma rekha, Bandha rekha or Kamala rekha; or on the lines of Fate, Life, Head or Apollo in Western palmistry.

Depending on where it is found on the hand, the Tree enhances the positive aspects of a line, and strengthens the potential for longevity, fame, wealth, brilliance or happiness.

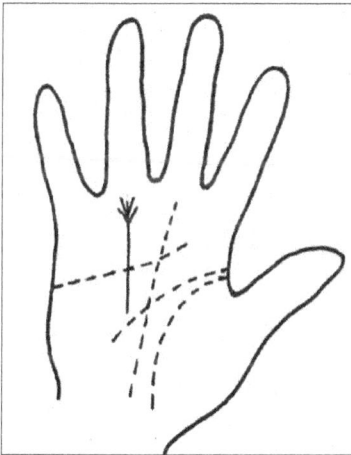

Figure 5.20. The Tree at the end of a line.

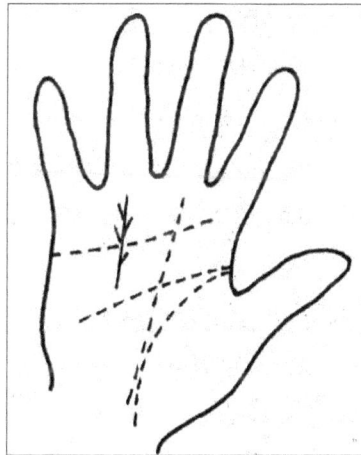

Figure 5.21. The Tree rising from a line.

The Triangle

Triangles can be either small or large. They are formed by three small independent lines or several larger ones.

In Hindu palmistry, a small triangle found on the Bandha rekha (Figure 5.22) reveals an individual who will enjoy success through his or her own efforts. When found on the Dhan rekha, it is a sign that the person will likely come into an inheritance.

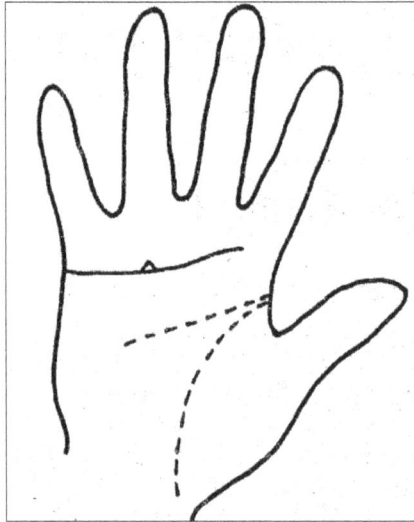

Figure 5.22. Small triangle on Bandha rekha.

Triangles located on the various *sthanas* have the following meanings in Indian palmistry:

- On Pithru sthana (Figure 5.23): skilled at diplomacy
- On Mathru sthana: attracted to mysticism; talented on occult sciences

- On Vidya sthana: strong talent in art and design
- On Jaya sthana: ability as a diplomat
- On Dharma sthana: talent in the martial arts
- On Brathru sthana or Bandhu sthana: person falls deeply in love with his or her partner

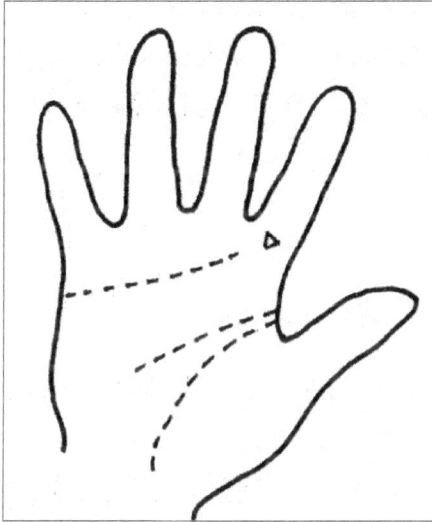

Figure 5.23. Triangle on Pithru sthana.

The Trident

Like the Tree mentioned earlier, the *Trident* can appear either independently (Figure 5.24) or at the end of another line (Figure 5.25). Considered rare by Indian palmists, it is a sign of good fortune, especially if it is clear and well-formed.

- When found on the end of the Kamala rekha on the Pithru sthana (Figure 5.24): the person will realize their aspirations in life

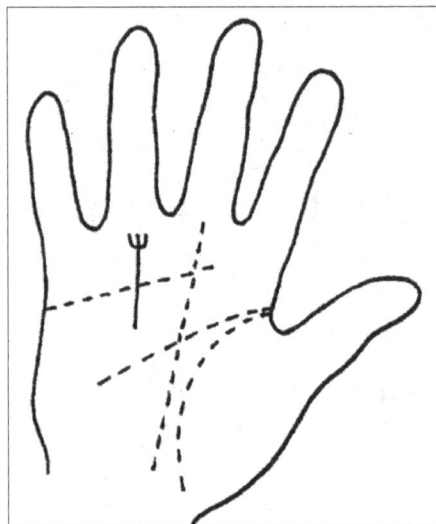

Figure 5.24. Trident at the end of Kamala rekha on Vidya sthana.

- When found on the Indira rekha, it is a sure indication of outstanding success or wealth at the age that it appears
- When located on the Vidya sthana (Figure 5.25): the owner will achieve a high degree of celebrity and renown

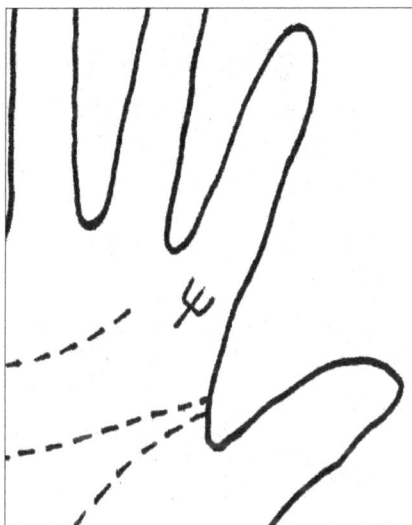

Figure 5.25. Trident on Pithru sthana.

The Yav

Taking the form of a small oval, the *yav* (or *yava*) can be found on the lower phalange of the thumb, on the Mani-Bandha rekha (Rascettes of Venus), on the joints of the fingers, and at the beginning or end of certain lines. Its appearance is not unlike a large island when found on a line.

- If found on the lower phalange of the thumb (Figure 5.26): material wealth and overall success in life
- If located at the base of the thumb (Figure 5.27): the person will have a son
- If found at the beginning of Indira rekha (Figure 5.28): death of parents at an early age

- If located at the end of Bandha rekha (Figure 5.29):
  the person will likely die at a holy place (such as in
  Varanasi, one of the holiest cities in India).

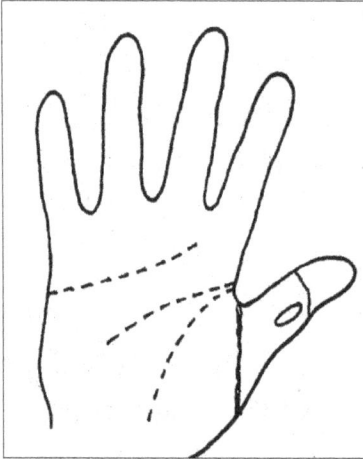

Figure 5.26. Yav on lower phalange of thumb.

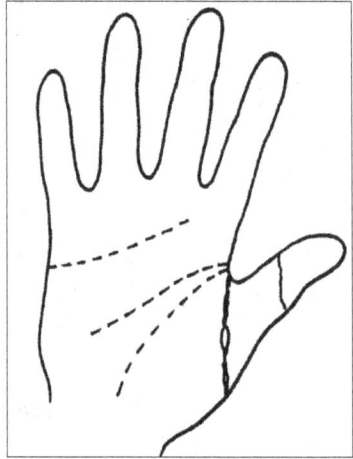

Figure 5.27. Yav on base of thumb.

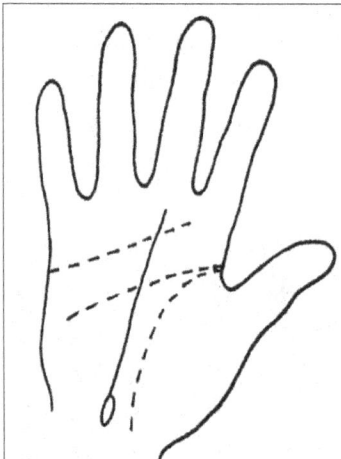

Figure 5.28. Yav at beginning of Indira rekha.

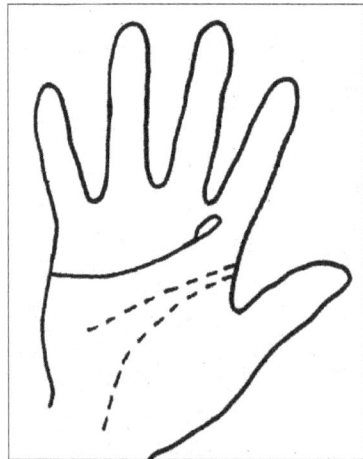

Figure 5.29. Yav at end of Bandha rekha.

For Further Study

Here are a few books that will deepen your knowledge about Indian palmistry. Many can be found on Amazon (India) and at Indian book stores, both in India and abroad.

Encyclopedia of Palm and Palm Reading by Dr. M. Katakkar (UBS Publishers' Distributors Ltd., 1992)

Your Destiny in Thumb by R.G. Rao (Ranjan Publications, 2014)

Samudrika Sudha by R.G. Rao (Sagar Publications, 2017)

All the Secrets of Palmistry by Dayanand Verma (Diamond Books, 2007)

Destiny in the Palm of Your Hand by Ghanshyam Singh Birla (Simon & Schuster, 2000)

Indian Palmistry by J.B. Dale (Srishti Publications, 2013)

Dictionary of Indian Palmistry Symbols by Sulabh Jain (Xlibris, 2017)

Palmistry: Sutra and Siddartha by Vinay Aditya (COE, Indian Council of Astrological Sciences, 2018)

Hast Samudrika Shastra by K.C. Sen (D.B. Taraporevala, 1960)

Ilm-ul-Kaff by M.M. Gaafar (D.B. Taraporevala, 1964)

Afterword

Hand analysis provides a master key to help us achieve self-awareness and understand our place in the universe. It teaches us that each individual temperament is a unique, equal and valid reflection of spiritual reality, and shows how it can be expressed in a positive and dynamic way from the core of our being.

Palmistry can guide us towards becoming aware of our hidden talents and aspirations, and can help us bridge the gap between our inner desires and outer reality. By taking responsibility for our life path, we can come into contact with what we really want on a deep level. Above all, hand analysis can inspire us to expand our inner vision. To the degree that we are able to release these positive unconscious forces, we are able to help others come upon their innate wisdom, joy and inner peace.

Indian palmistry is one of the three major world schools of palmistry, which include the Chinese school and the Western school, which is believed to have originated in the Middle East. It is hoped that this slim volume will create more interest in Indian palmistry, and inspire the reader to further study.

About the Author

Nathaniel Altman is a Brooklyn-based writer, teacher and hand analyst who has authored more than twenty books on spirituality, peace studies, healthy diets, alternative healing, nature and relationship.

First introduced to Indian palmistry in 1976, Nathaniel has been reading hands since 1969 after developing an interest in palmistry while studying in South America. He soon began reading the hands of everyone he knew, and started taking prints of the hands of family members and friends. This has grown to a collection of thousands of handprints. Nathaniel's hobby gradually developed into a profession. Over the years he has read the hands of over 25,000 individuals, including those he has met at a wide variety of corporate events sponsored by Martha Stewart Omnimedia, Time Warner, HBO, American Lawyer Media, Avon, Merrill Lynch, The New York Times Company, Dr. Pepper, Bloomberg, Cravath, Swaine & Moore, The Whitney Museum of American Art, McKinsey & Company, Mail.com, America Online and others.

Nathaniel has authored or co-authored numerous books about palmistry, including *The Palmistry Workbook* (The Aquarian Press, 1982); *Sexual Palmistry* (The Aquarian Press, 1984, Adams Media, 2002, Gaupo Publishing, 2019); *Palmistry, Career and Self-Fulfillment* (with Andrew Fitzherbert, published by The Aquarian Press in 1988); *Medical Palmistry* (with Eugene Scheimann, M.D., published by The Aquarian Press in 1989); and *The Little Giant Encyclopedia of Palmistry*

(Sterling Publishing, 1999). The original edition of *Palmistry: The Universal Guide* was published by Sterling in 2009, and published in a new edition by Gaupo Publishing in 2017.

Nathaniel's palmistry titles have been translated into more than a dozen languages, including Spanish, Portuguese, Greek, Dutch, Arabic, Serbian, Hebrew, Estonian, Swedish, Finnish, Thai, Italian, German, Russian and Chinese.

A 1971 graduate of the University of Wisconsin in Madison, Nathaniel served as a faculty member at the Krotona School of Theosophy in Ojai, California and as coordinator of the International Theosophical Youth Centre in Adyar, India. He has appeared on over 150 radio and television programs throughout the United States, Australia, Latin America and Europe. Nathaniel's articles have been featured in a variety of publications, including *Good Housekeeping, Natural Health, Well Being, Free Spirit, New Life, USA Today* and *Vegetarian Times.*

Nathaniel's personal website can be found at http://www.nathanielaltman.com.

Index

Hara rekha, 53-54

Hast Samudrika Shastra, 3

Head line; *see* Dhan rekha

Heart line; *see* Bandha rekha

Healing ability, 30

Hemavalli rekha, 52

Hridgata-hatwada; *see* Jaya rekha

Incarnations, 1, 35

Index finger, 27, 29, 30, 64, 65

Indira rekha, 42-23, 49, 55, 56, 73, 76, 79, 81, 83, 87, 90, 91, 92

Influence lines, 58

Islands, 62, 79-80

Jaya rekha, 58, 79, 80

Jaya sthana, 16, 40, 74, 78, 85, 89

Kamahhastika rekha, 49-50

Kamala rekha, 44, 74, 87, 90

Kanishthra rekha, 58

Kartikeyan system of palmistry, 14, 15, 45

Korpara rekha, 50, 51

Krishna, Lord, 18

Kumar, Nitin, 35, 37

Kuthor rekha, 85-86

Leadership ability, 76

Life line; *see* Atma rekha

Lines, *see also* individual *rekhas*

major, 34-46

Of Related Interest

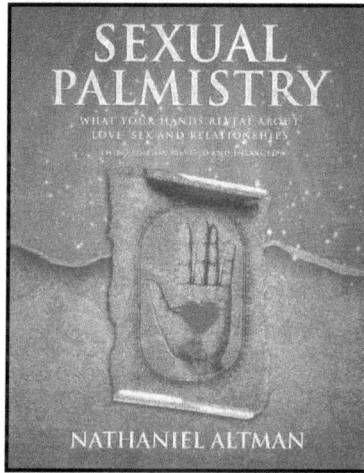

Chinese Palmistry: A Short Treatise

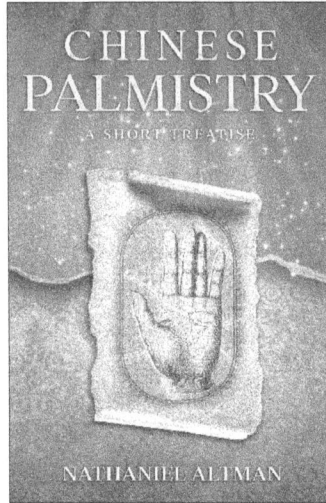

The Chinese have been studying hands for thousands of years. Originally a spiritual practice to understand the mysteries of existence, palmistry remains extremely popular among Chinese today to achieve self-knowledge and to enable them to make decisions about the future. Chinese palmistry focuses on "the five elements" hand types, as well as the fingers, thenar elevations (palaces) and lines that make up the human hand. It also evaluates the meanings of skin texture and temperature, hand size and flexibility as well as small markings on the palm. As a companion volume to *Indian Palmistry*, *Chinese Palmistry* provides a basic introduction to this fascinating study. Trade paperback (6" x 9"), 2020.

Gaupo Publishing
Brooklyn, New York
www.gaupo.net

www.ingramcontent.com/pod-product-compliance
Lightning Source LLC
Chambersburg PA
CBHW060818050426
42449CB00008B/1720